GREAT EVENTS

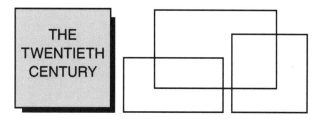

THE TWENTIETH CENTURY

GREAT EVENTS

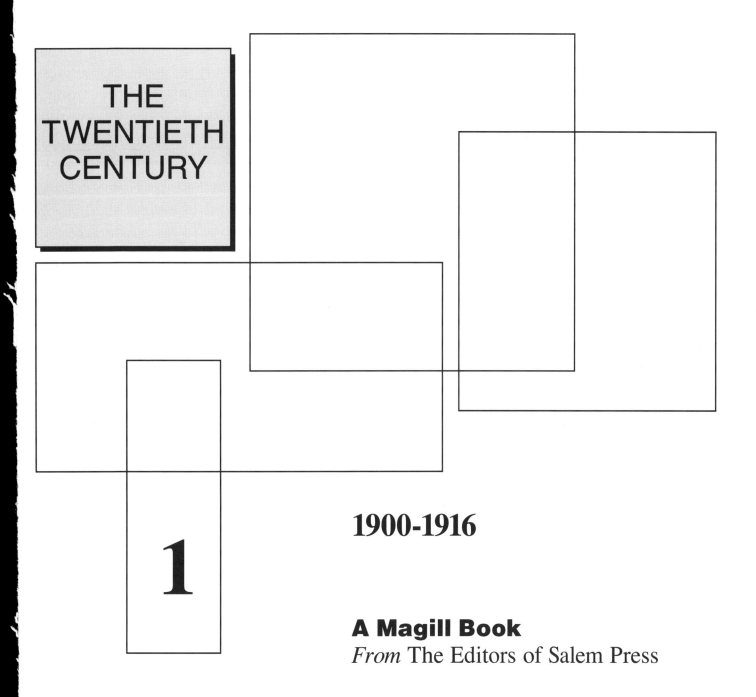

THE TWENTIETH CENTURY

1900-1916

1

A Magill Book

From The Editors of Salem Press

SALEM PRESS, INC.

Pasadena, California   Englewood Cliffs, New Jersey

Library of Congress Cataloging-in-Publication Data

Great events.
     v. cm. — (The Twentieth Century)
   "A Magill book from the editors of Salem Press."
   Includes indexes.
   Summary: Surveys significant events in the history of civil rights, military conflicts, economics, international relations, legislation, and social reform in the twentieth century.
    1. History, Modern—20th century. I. Salem Press. II. Series: Twentieth century (Pasadena, Calif.)
D422.G72   1992
909.82—dc20   92-28671
ISBN 0-89356-796-5 (set)   CIP
ISBN 0-89356-797-3 (volume 1)   AC

Second Printing

PUBLISHER'S NOTE

The Twentieth Century: Great Events is the second in a new series of reference books from Salem Press. The first twenty volumes, *Great Athletes*, surveys more than seven hundred major twentieth century sports champions from around the world, representing more than forty different sports. Like *Great Athletes*, the ten volumes of *Great Events* offers a comprehensive overview of its topic in a format that combines text and photographs to present subject matter that is both inviting to the eye and engaging to readers from the middle-school level on up.

Great Events offers 472 articles, arranged in chronological order from 1900 to 1992, covering major turning points in the history of international events: wars and other military conflicts, from the Boxer Rebellion through the battles of the two world wars to Korea, Vietnam, and conflicts of the post-Cold War era; economics, from the early twentieth century dollar diplomacy of President Taft to the global recession of the late century, felt especially in Russia as it moves into a market economy; landmark legislation in civil rights and social reform (e.g., *Brown* v. *Board of Education*, *Roe* v. *Wade*, the anti-apartheid developments in South Africa); the trend toward independent nations and ethnicities, from the revolutions in Africa to more recent overthrow of oppressive Eastern European regimes in favor of more democratic political systems; and other major developments in international relations: the Law of the Sea treaty, the Helsinki Agreement, the reopening of U.S.-Chinese relations, the reunification of the two Germanys, the dissolution of the Communist world of Russia and Eastern Europe, and the disintegration of the Yugoslav republics, to name only a few. The types of event covered, therefore, scrutinize the "macro" historical developments of our century: those political, economic, and social movements that have affected the course of civilization at the level of nations as well as of individuals. Milestones of science and technology, on the one hand, and of the arts and popular culture, on the other, will be addressed in subsequent publications in this series.

Each article provides the ready-reference data for which Magill books have come to be known over the years: Beginning with a headline-title which announces the event (such as "Indira Gandhi Is Assassinated"), the front matter goes on to describe the event and define its significance in a brief (boxed and italicized) sentence. There follows a list of the "What," "When," "Where," and "Who" of the event, providing both young students and adults with the vital data within the first page. The text of each article is divided into three subsections, the first and second of which detail the event itself and its background, and the last of which, "Consequences," identifies the long-range impact of the event. Accompanying the text is a photograph depicting the event itself or a key personage connected with it.

The chronological arrangement of the articles not only serves as a massive time line but also casts some light on the socio-politico-economic evolution of our world from a collection of individual nations to a global community, in which developments in one region have inevitable repercussions in others. A more compact Time Line is the last article in volume 10. To allow the extraction of information about a particular topic or person, five indexes provide more access to the events: a Chronological Index, providing the contents for all volumes in one place; an Alphabetical Key Word Index, identifying major terms and concepts; a Category Index, in which each article appears under the major area or areas — such as "Politics and Political Reform" or "Military Conflict" — to which it applies; a Personages Index, which lists all major figures found in the "Who" section of each article; and a Geographical Index, in which the articles are arranged by the countries involved. For convenience' sake, all these indexes appear in each volume.

Many hands went into the creation of this work, from the academicians who contributed articles (a list of whom appears in volume 1) to the editors who researched information and selected photographs to illustrate the entries. Special thanks are extended to Ruth Goring Stewart for copy- and line-editing, and to Susan Hormuth for photo research. Their efforts are gratefully acknowledged.

Amy Adelstein
J. Stewart Alverson
Stephen E. Ambrose
David L. Ammerman
Robert R. Archibald
Paul Ashin
Bryan Aubrey
Abdulla K. Badsha
James A. Baer
JoAnn Balingit
Terry Alan Baney
Iraj Bashiri
Erving E. Beauregard
Patricia A. Behlar
Meredith William Berg
S. Carol Berg
Arthur Blaser
Arnold Blumberg
James J. Bolner
Jo-Ellen Lipman Boon
Gordon L. Bowen
Anita O. Bowser
Michael R. Bradley
John A. Britton
Kathleen S. Britton
John R. Broadus
Kendall W. Brown
M. Leann Brown
Dallas L. Browne
Anthony R. Brunello
Maurice P. Brungardt
Henry H. Bucher, Jr.
Jack L. Calbert
Laura M. Calkins
Edmund J. Campion

Sheila Carapico
Diane K. Chary
Frederick B. Chary
Peng-Khuan Chong
Ronald J. Cima
Donald N. Clark
John G. Clark
Richard H. Collin
Robert O. Collins
Bernard A. Cook
Charles E. Cottle
David H. Culbert
Merle O. Davis
Roger P. Davis
John H. DeBerry
E. Gene DeFelice
Tyler Deierhoi
Charles A. Desnoyers
Mustafah Dhada
Thomas I. Dickson
Daniel D. DiPiazza
Fredrick J. Dobney
David Leonard Downie
John Duffy
Samuel K. Eddy
Rand Edwards
Barry Faye
Elizabeth Fee
James E. Fickle
John W. Fiero
George J. Fleming
George Q. Flynn
Richard G. Frederick
Richard A. Fredland
Jonathan M. Furdek

John C. Gardner
Roger A. Geimer
Larry N. George
Leonard H. D. Gordon
Robert F. Gorman
John H. Greising
Alan G. Gross
Manfred Grote
John J. Grotpeter
James M. Haas
John R. Hanson II
William Harrigan
Fred R. van Hartesveldt
Glenn Hastedt
Louis D. Hayes
Hans Heilbronner
Peter B. Heller
Mary A. Hendrickson
Howard M. Hensel
Hames J. Herlan
James F. Hitchcock
Donald Holley
Cabot C. Holmes
Mahmood Ibrahim
Robert Jacobs
Andrew Jamison
Charles W. Johnson
Joseph S. Joseph
Richard C. Kagan
Edward Kannyo
Christopher J. Kauffman
Burton Kaufman
Edward P. Keleher
Rodney D. Keller
Clive Kileff

Barry L. Knight

Paul W. Knoll

Gregory C. Kozlowski

Felicia Krishna-Hensel

Richard L. Langill

Michael M. Laskier

Saul Lerner

Thomas T. Lewis

Roger D. Long

William C. Lowe

Arthur L. Lowrie

Arthur F. McClure

James Edward McGoldrick

Paul D. Mageli

Russell M. Magnaghi

Cynthia Keppley Mahmood

Renée Marlin-Bennett

Paul T. Mason

Thomas D. Matijasic

Daniel J. Meissner

Joan E. Meznar

George R. Mitchell

Paul Monaco

Rex O. Mooney

Lincoln R. Mui

Vidya Nadkarni

Veronica Nmoma

Burl L. Noggle

Norma C. Noonan

Robert C. Oberst

Kenneth O'Reilly

Judith A. Parsons

Jerry A. Pattengale

Thomas R. Peake

Samuel C. Pearson

William A. Pelz

Louis G. Perez

Doris F. Pierce

Francis Poole

Philip R. Popple

James W. Pringle

George F. Putnam

John D. Raymer

Dennis Reinhartz

Richard Rice

Karl A. Roider

Courtney B. Ross

Frank Louis Rusciano

José M. Sánchez

Eve N. Sandberg

Richard H. Sander

Wayne D. Santoni

J. Christopher Schnell

Harold A. Schofield

Margaret S. Schoon

Thomas C. Schunk

Catherine V. Scott

Asit Kumar Sen

L. B. Shriver

R. Baird Shuman

Michael S. Smith

Ira Smolensky

Beatrice Spade

Ronald N. Spector

Leon Stein

James H. Steinel

Ruth Goring Stewart

J. K. Sweeney

Renée Taft

Carol Whyte Talabay

Emory M. Thomas

Jack Ray Thomas

Larry Thornton

Paul B. Trescott

Anne Trotter

William M. Tuttle

Jiu-Hwa Lo Upshur

Jonathan G. Utley

Stuart Van Dyke, Jr.

Indu Vohra

Harry E. Wade

Shirley Ann Wagner

Bennett H. Wall

Martha Ellen Webb

T. K. Welliver

Allen Wells

Mary C. Wendel

Paul A. Whelan

Thomas L. Whigham

Theodore A. Wilson

John D. Windhausen

Frank Wu

Edward A. Zivich

CONTENTS

GREAT EVENTS

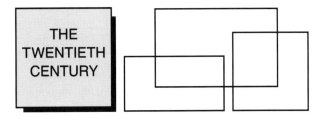

THE
TWENTIETH
CENTURY

U.S. REFORMS EXTEND THE VOTE

Various laws and amendments adopted by individual states and by Congress gave common people a greater share in government decision making.

The Need for Change

The U.S. Declaration of Independence affirmed that all men are created equal, and in the middle of the nineteenth century Abraham Lincoln said that government must be "of the people, by the people, and for the people." Still, even at the beginning of the twentieth century the American voting system fell short of these ideals.

By 1890, the right to vote had been extended to all adult male citizens. Only in a few Western states, however, were women allowed the same right. United States senators were elected by state legislatures rather than by the people, and there were no legal means for people to impeach public officials — to seek to remove elected persons from office because of misconduct. Moreover, voters had no way of forcing state legislatures to take action on specific issues.

Under the common system of casting votes, ballots of different colors were printed by the political parties or independent candidates and were distributed to the voters. As voters deposited their ballots in the appropriate boxes, they were watched by their employers or people who held local political power. Clearly, this system encouraged fraud and bribery: Some officials bought people's votes, and employers could threaten employees with the loss of their jobs if they did not vote as the employers wished.

Candidates were generally chosen in party caucuses — gatherings dominated by a wealthy few. The common citizen had no say in the choice of candidates whose names appeared on the ballot. Because there were no controls on campaign spending, the rich had great influence over the

What: Civil rights
When: 1900-1913
Where: The United States
Who:
STEPHEN GROVER CLEVELAND (1837-1908), President of the United States from 1885 to 1889 and 1893 to 1897
ROBERT MARION LAFOLLETTE (1855-1925), Governor of Wisconsin from 1901 to 1906
WILLIAM U'REN (1859-1949), a newspaper editor from Oregon who has been called "the father of direct democracy"

course of political campaigns. In 1907, when Simon Guggenheim revealed publicly what he had spent to get elected U.S. Senator from Colorado, the nation was shocked. Many agreed that the system needed to be changed.

Reforms and Reformers

The secret ballot (also called the Australian ballot) had been first introduced in the state of Massachusetts in 1888. Through the efforts of President Grover Cleveland and others, this system had come into nationwide use by the election of 1910. Now voters could make choices according to their convictions, without being pressured by their employers or others.

Under the leadership of Governor Robert LaFollette, the state of Wisconsin pioneered the use of primaries to select those who would run in

the general election. In this way voters gained a voice in the nomination of candidates. The primary system soon spread across the country.

In the first decade of the twentieth century, more and more states gave women the vote and enacted other important reforms. Laws designed to curb corrupt election practices and to limit campaign spending came onto the books in many states, and similar federal laws followed.

Oregon was a leader in the movement to make voting a true exercise of democracy. A key figure in the movement was William U'Ren, who never held a major political office yet was responsible for significant reforms in Oregon and ultimately across the United States. A blacksmith who later became a newspaper editor and a lawyer, U'Ren had read how "direct democracy" was practiced in Switzerland and committed himself to introducing it in his state. Mostly as a result of his efforts, Oregon adopted the initiative and referendum in 1902, the direct primary in 1904, and the recall in 1910.

Initiative and referendum made it possible for a majority vote among the people — the electorate — to pass laws when the legislature was unable or unwilling to do so. They also gave voters the power to veto unpopular laws. With the power of recall, voters could quickly remove an elected official if they were displeased with his conduct.

Recall was adopted more readily by states west of the Mississippi. Eastern states, usually more conservative, did not generally favor recall but did come to adopt initiative and referendum.

During this same period, there was a drive to amend the U.S. Constitution to allow a direct vote for U.S. senators. Across the country many had become aware that because the Senate was not answerable to the people, it had turned into a "rich men's club" that had opposed many progressive laws, such as those abolishing child labor and revising the tariff system.

Western states were again in the forefront of the movement toward change. Several of them began holding primary elections to select Senate nominees, and in some of these states there were laws forcing the state legislature to abide by the voters' choices. By 1912, twenty-nine states had adopted this way of giving the voters greater power. Finally, the Senate submitted a constitutional amendment to the states for ratification. The Seventeenth Amendment, providing for direct election of senators, was ratified on May 31, 1913.

Consequences

With the ratification of the Seventeenth Amendment, a number of major political reforms were in place across the United States. Though the guarantee of all women citizens' right to vote would have to await the passage of the Nineteenth Amendment in 1920, many states, particularly those in the West, were establishing that right within their borders. Through the secret ballot, the primary, the initiative, the referendum, the recall, and laws limiting campaign spending, political power was placed in the hands of American voters as it never had been before.

A political convention, early twentieth century. (*Library of Congress*)

The Boxer Rebellion Fails to Remove Foreign Control in China

> With the Boxer Rebellion, the Chinese people tried to free themselves from the influence and control of foreigners.

What: Civil strife
When: June-September, 1900
Where: North China, especially Shantung and Chihli provinces
Who:
Tz'u-hsi (1835-1908), Empress Dowager of China
Kuang-hsü (1871-1908), Emperor of China from 1875 to 1908
Count Alfred von Waldersee (1832-1904), commander of the international force sent to China

Staking Claims in China

After the First Opium War with Great Britain (1839-1842), China was pressured more and more by foreign powers. Foreigners were given the rights to control trade, collect customs money, and run the courts in dozens of Chinese cities, called "Treaty Ports."

After Hong Kong was given to the British in 1842, wars and threats forced the Ch'ing (Manchu) Dynasty to give up other territories. Russia had special influence in Manchuria and Central Asia; France took control of Indochina in 1884; and Japan humiliated China in a war in 1894 and took Taiwan as a prize. Soon Germany was also competing for influence in China.

Sometimes the Chinese tried to rise up against this foreign domination, but the empire's armies and ocean fleets were no match for the military forces of foreign powers. In the 1890's, many secret societies and militia worked to oppose foreigners—especially in the northern provinces of Chihli, Shantung, and Shensi, where there were many Christian missionaries and other foreigners.

Some of the most active secret societies were part of the I-ho Ch'üan (Association of Righteousness and Harmony, usually called the "Righteous and Harmonious Fists"). In its ceremonies, this group practiced the ancient Chinese art of *t'ai-chi ch'uan*, which included shadowboxing. Thus the foreigners nicknamed this group the "Boxers."

The Boxers had always been opposed to foreign control. In fact, at first they worked against the Ch'ing Dynasty, because the Manchus (who had founded the dynasty and still held most of the important court positions) did not come from the Han ethnic group. More and more, however, the Boxers began to oppose missionaries—especially after the Germans started dominating Shantung in 1898.

Reform and Rebellion

The Ch'ing government was in a difficult position. The Boxers and other groups wanted foreigners out, while the foreign powers insisted that the government stand firm against the Boxers.

For a short time in the summer of 1898, it seemed as if some of the problems would be resolved. Emperor Kuang-hsü, who had recently come of age, began to reform the Chinese government. In September, however, this "One Hundred Days of Reform" came to a sudden end. Kuang-

Chinese "Boxer" c. 1900. (*National Archives*)

hsü's aunt, Empress Dowager Tz'u-hsi, and her chief adviser, Jung-lu, staged a coup. Kuang-hsü was arrested, and Tz'u-hsi became ruler of China. She was committed to getting rid of foreign control.

With the support of many officials in North China, the Boxers began to attack foreign railroads and settlements. Their motto became "Fu-Ch'ing, mieh-yang" (support the Ch'ing, exterminate the foreigners). During the winter of

1899-1900, the foreign powers in China protested the Boxers' attacks and began threatening to send troops.

The Empress Dowager believed the Boxers when they claimed that the foreigners' bullets could not harm them, and she called upon the army and people to defend the country from a foreign invasion that was sure to come. Now the Boxers in Peking (Beijing), Chihli, and Shensi joined the fight. Hundreds of missionaries and thousands of Chinese Christians were tortured and killed.

In early June, a force of foreign troops sent from Tientsin was turned back by Boxers and Chinese army units. The German minister to China, Count Clemens von Kettler, was shot down in the streets of the capital. On June 21, 1900, the Ch'ing government declared war on all the treaty powers in China. The Boxer militia was commanded to attack the section of Peking where the foreign diplomats lived.

Chinese officials throughout the empire were told to cooperate with the Boxers in attacking foreigners. Those in North China obeyed, but government and army leaders in many other parts of the country did their best to avoid open attacks. Some of them felt sympathy for the captive emperor or doubted the Boxers' fighting abilities.

By late July, a powerful international force of twenty thousand men—including Germans, Japanese, Americans, British, Russians, French, Austrians, and Italians—had been brought together in Tientsin under the command of Count Alfred von Waldersee. After two weeks of fighting, they made their way to Peking, entered the city through an unguarded sewer gate, and ended the siege of the diplomatic section.

The Empress Dowager and her court fled to Sian, and most government forces surrendered quickly. The Boxers, who had not proved reliable in battle, escaped to the countryside of North China.

Angry at the Boxers' cruel treatment of for-eigners and Chinese Christians, the allied troops began looting and burning the suburbs of Peking and Tientsin. International forces occupied the capital until September, 1901, and the Empress Dowager did not return until the beginning of 1902.

The final peace treaty, the Boxer Protocols, was accepted by the Chinese on January 16, 1901. Under the treaty, officials who had cooperated with the Boxers were to be dismissed, exiled, or even executed. Foreigners were to occupy the area between Peking and Tientsin, and China was to pay $333 million in war reparations over a period of thirty-nine years.

Consequences

Because of the Boxer Rebellion, the Ch'ing Dynasty lost the respect of the Chinese people as well as the respect of foreign powers. Many people with skills and education avoided serving a government that seemed so incompetent. Nationalism became a stronger force among the Chinese people, especially in Chinese communities overseas.

The empire had severe money problems. Its income was not enough to pay the war debt, so taxes had to be increased, and loans were taken from banks in Western countries.

The Empress Dowager now reluctantly opened the way for many of the "Hundred Days" reforms. Education was modernized, along with army training. Chinese officials toured the West, studying the different systems of government. They made a plan for a constitutional monarchy in China, and there were elections in 1909 and 1910 for regional and national parliaments.

For a number of young Chinese, however, these reforms came too late. A number of republican, nationalist, reform, and secret society organizations joined in the Revolutionary Alliance, led by Sun Yat-sen. This coalition managed to topple the empire on October 10, 1911.

THE COMMONWEALTH OF AUSTRALIA AND THE DOMINION OF NEW ZEALAND ARE BORN

Australia and New Zealand, which had been British colonies, became self-governing states.

Australia Becomes a Federation

Though both the United States and Australia were once colonies of Great Britain, their paths to self-government were quite different. The British government had not wanted the American colonies to become independent, but the American people rose up and fought to win their freedom. After the humiliation of being forced to yield control of the thirteen North American colonies, British policy toward its colonies changed. Throughout the nineteenth century, when other British colonies populated by white settlers sought independence, the government of Great Britain was generally cooperative.

The Canadian colonies, which became the Dominion of Canada in 1867, benefited first from this new approach. Australia was next. Neither these countries nor New Zealand had to fight a revolutionary war to gain freedom from Great Britain's control.

What is now Australia had become home to several diverse groups of people. Its original inhabitants were wandering bands of aborigines. The first settlers from abroad were English and Irish convicts whose punishment was forced exile to this large island. When gold was discovered there in 1851, a great wave of British immigrants came of their own accord to seek a share of the new wealth. By 1889, the island had been divided into six colonies: Victoria, New South Wales, Queensland, South Australia, Tasmania, and Western Australia.

In February, 1890, premiers of the six colonies gathered in Melbourne to discuss the possibility

What: Political independence
When: 1901, 1907
Where: Australia, New Zealand, and Great Britain
Who:
SIR EDMUND BARTON (1849-1920), first Prime Minister of the Australian Federation
SIR GEORGE HOUSTON REID (1845-1918), Premier of New South Wales from 1894 to 1899
SIR JOSEPH GEORGE WARD (1856-1930), Premier of New Zealand from 1906 to 1912
JOSEPH CHAMBERLAIN (1836-1914), British Secretary of State for the Colonies from 1895 to 1903
VICTOR ALEXANDER BRUCE, NINTH EARL OF ELGIN (1849-1917), British Secretary of State for the Colonies from 1905 to 1908

of federation—uniting under a central government that would permit each colony (or state) a degree of independence. The colonial legislatures sent delegates to the first Australasian Convention a year later, in March, 1891, in Sydney. In April the convention approved a draft constitution for a federal system of government.

Yet the colonial legislatures were not enthusiastic about the proposed constitution and did not take any action on it. Those who were involved in the growing trade-union movement thought the

7

constitution would not give enough power to the common people; others said it took too many powers away from the individual colonies.

Within each colony, however, there were "Federal Leagues" keeping alive the vision of an Australian federation. In August, 1894, George Houston Reid, Premier of New South Wales, called for another conference of premiers to plan a new constitutional convention. The conference of premiers, which met in Hobart, Tasmania, in January, 1895, decided that this time the delegates who would draft a constitution would be elected by the people in each of the six colonies. The resulting constitution would be put to a popular vote in each colony, and once approved by the people, it would be submitted to the British government for final approval.

Elections for constitutional delegates were held in every colony except Queensland. The federal constitution convention began on March 22,

1897, in Adelaide, and concluded on March 17, 1898, in Melbourne. The rivalry between smaller, poorer colonies and those that were larger and wealthier caused most of the convention's controversy. Finally, however, a draft constitution was put together and brought before the voters of each colony.

Amendments to safeguard the interests of New South Wales, the largest colony, were needed before the new constitution could receive enough votes in all colonies. Finally, however, the document was ready to be presented to the British Colonial Secretary, Joseph Chamberlain, and other officials in London.

Chamberlain introduced the necessary legislation in the British Parliament, and on July 9, 1900, Queen Victoria signed the new act creating the Commonwealth of Australia. On January 1, 1901, Edmund Barton was appointed as its first prime minister.

New Zealand Follows Suit

The two islands of New Zealand were originally inhabited by the Maoris, a people related to the Polynesians. The first British settlers were mostly traders, adventurers, and shipwrecked sailors. Though Great Britain annexed the islands in 1840, the Maoris launched wars against the white colonists, and it was not until 1870 that the British Army finally crushed the resistance.

Beginning in 1856, New Zealand's government was appointed by the British governor, but it was responsible to the popularly elected branch of the legislature. Twenty years later, further political reforms took power away from the provincial governments and gave it to a central administration. With regard to internal affairs, New Zealand had become fully self-governing.

For the most part, the New Zealanders were quite loyal to Great Britain; still, a desire for independence grew among them. They were beginning to see themselves as a country separate from England. Their government began to claim larger rights, such as the right to negotiate trade agreements with foreign states. Another step toward full independence came when Premier Richard Seddon proclaimed New Zealand's annexation of the Cook Islands, in 1901.

Premiers of all the self-governing British colonies gathered in London in 1907, at what was called the Imperial Conference. There New Zealand's premier, Sir Joseph Ward, urged the British government to change the official status of New Zealand from that of a "colony" to that of a "dominion."

British Colonial Secretary Victor Alexander Bruce, Lord Elgin, realized that his government could continue to count on New Zealand's support of its interests. After all, New Zealand had voluntarily sent troops to fight on Great Britain's side in the Boer War of 1899-1902 in southern Africa. Ward obtained ready agreement from Lord Elgin and other British officials, and when he returned home, the New Zealand Parliament gave its formal approval to the change in name. It would be known from that time onward as the Dominion of New Zealand.

Consequences

Australia and New Zealand achieved independence from Great Britain through a process of negotiation rather than war. Ties of loyalty to the British Empire remained. Both countries fought on the side of Great Britain in World War I and World War II. Yet their military and economic ties gradually weakened throughout the twentieth century, as the Empire disintegrated and new alliances were formed. Today, what special ties remain between Australia and New Zealand and their "mother country" are ties of language and culture, not governmental and economic control.

Settlers on a New Zealand homestead. (*Library of Congress*)

The Insular Cases Determine Status of U.S. Possessions Overseas

Supreme Court decisions about whether tariff laws were applicable to overseas possessions of the United States helped clarify the status of such territories as Puerto Rico, the Philippines, and the Virgin Islands.

What: Law
When: May 27, 1901
Where: Washington, D.C.
Who:
Henry Billings Brown (1836-1913), Associate Justice of the United States from 1890 to 1906
Edward Douglass White (1845-1921), Associate Justice of the United States from 1894 to 1910
Melville Weston Fuller (1833-1910), Chief Justice of the United States from 1888 to 1910

New Colonies, New Problems

From its founding through the nineteenth century, the United States expanded across the North American continent. Through the annexation and settlement of new territories, the nation gradually added states. The problems and questions that arose often had to do with states' rights versus the rights of the federal government.

In 1898, however, the United States suddenly became a colonial power. Through a joint resolution of Congress, Hawaii was annexed; at the end of the Spanish-American War, Spain ceded Puerto Rico, Guam, and the Philippine Islands to the United States as well.

With these new overseas possessions came new questions. Was it right for the United States to acquire overseas territories at all? If it was consti-tutionally and ethically allowed, how should such territories be governed? Did the rights guaranteed to Americans under the Constitution apply to these lands and their people? The Constitution required, for example, that all taxes, duties, and imposts be uniform throughout the United States. Did that apply to overseas colonies as well?

Those who opposed American imperialism adopted a slogan, "The Constitution follows the flag." Wherever the United States governed, they argued, the Constitution had to be in force. If a territory had no prospect of becoming a full-fledged state, it should not be annexed. Opponents of imperialism—mainly Democrats—believed that under the Constitution, the federal government did not have the power to take over land that would be held permanently as a colony. Colonialism, they said, was in contradiction to the Declaration of Independence itself.

Supporters of colonial expansion—mostly Republicans—said that the United States, by winning the Spanish-American War, had already become a world power. Overseas possessions would strengthen the nation's military security and give it more control of the seas. Furthermore, the colonies could help the United States gain economic strength.

The Court's Decisions

The Supreme Court became part of the debate when it heard the "Insular Tariff Cases" for six days in January, 1901, and announced its opinions on May 27, 1901.

Henry Billings Brown. (*Library of Congress*)

DeLima v. *Bidwell* had to do with whether general tariff laws applied to imports from Puerto Rico once the treaty with Spain had been signed and Puerto Rico had become a U.S. territory. Should the normal tariffs on overseas imports be levied on goods coming from Puerto Rico? In stating the majority opinion, Justice Henry Billings Brown said, "We are therefore of the opinion that at the time these duties were levied, Puerto Rico was not a foreign country within the meaning of the tariff laws but a territory of the United States, that the duties were illegally exacted and that the plaintiffs are entitled to recover them back." Four of the nine justices, however, dissented from this opinion, insisting that Puerto Rico was not "a part" of the United States and so the tariff laws still applied.

The companion case, *Downes* v. *Bidwell*, had to do with whether a special tariff law applicable only to Puerto Rican goods (the Foraker Act) was valid. Though the decision in this case seems to contradict the *DeLima* v. *Bidwell* decision, Justice Brown again delivered the majority opinion. He took up not only the question of the tariff but also the larger issue of the constitutionality of colonization. The courts, he said, should be careful not to put obstacles in the way of the "American Empire." It might be desirable to annex distant possessions "inhabited by alien races, differing from us in religion, customs, laws, methods of taxation and modes of thought." Treating such possessions differently from states, he said, was not forbidden in the Constitution. He went on to rule that Puerto Rico belonged to the United States but was not "a part" of the United States. The Foraker Act, then, was constitutional.

Justice Edward Douglass White wrote an opinion in support of Brown's. In this opinion he explained his theory of "incorporation," which later came to be generally accepted by the Court. Though Puerto Rico did belong to the United States, he said, it had not been "incorporated"

into the nation, so the Constitution did not apply to it.

Chief Justice Melville Weston Fuller wrote a dissenting opinion, supported by three other justices. The Constitution did follow the flag, he claimed, and Puerto Rico should not be subject to special taxes or tariffs.

Later cases took up questions of the rights of criminal defendants in the territories. Was the Bill of Rights in force for the inhabitants of overseas colonies? In *Hawaii* v. *Mankichi* (1903), Justice Brown said that it was not in force for Hawaii at that time. In Hawaii, then, a defendant could be convicted by only nine "guilty" votes out of a jury of twelve. On the basis of his "incorporation" theory, Justice White agreed.

In 1905, the Court decided that Alaska had been "incorporated" into the United States to the extent that its people did enjoy constitutional guarantees. In the *Rasmussen* v. *United States* case, then, the Court reversed the conviction of an Alaskan defendant found guilty on the basis of a six-member jury. The Court continued to make these kinds of distinctions. Though Congress had granted U.S. citizenship to Puerto Ricans, the Court ruled in 1918 (*Puerto Rico* v. *Tapia*) that these citizens were not necessarily protected by the Constitution.

Consequences

The Insular Cases, in effect, gave Supreme Court approval to the United States' pursuit of overseas empire. Until they were "incorporated," these colonies and their people were not guaranteed constitutional rights.

Alaska and Hawaii, the two territories that were found by the Supreme Court to have been incorporated, became states of the Union in 1959 and 1960, respectively. The Philippines, Puerto Rico, and the Virgin Islands never were incorporated, though their inhabitants were declared U.S. citizens.

THEODORE ROOSEVELT ASSUMES THE U.S. PRESIDENCY

Taking up the United States presidency after the fatal shooting of William McKinley, Theodore Roosevelt brought new energy and prestige to the office.

Inheriting the Office

In Buffalo, New York, on September 6, 1901, an anarchist named Leon Czolgosz shot and seriously wounded William McKinley, President of the United States. Rushing to the side of the stricken president, Vice President Theodore Roosevelt was reassured that though the wound was severe, McKinley would probably recover.

Thinking to communicate this reassurance to the American people through his actions, Roosevelt left for a mountain-climbing expedition in New York's Adirondacks. While still in the mountains, he received a report by special messenger that the president was dying. By buckboard and train, Roosevelt hurried back to Buffalo but was unable to reach the city before McKinley's death. On the afternoon of September 14, 1901, Theodore Roosevelt took the oath of office as President of the United States.

It was a dramatic beginning for a dramatic career. As he faced his new responsibilities, Roosevelt's situation was not easy. He had risen to the presidency through a tragedy, not by the vote of the people. He was a Republican, but the Republican Party did not by any means promise its full support. In fact, Senator Marcus A. Hanna of Ohio, who had been President McKinley's chief supporter, seemed to be planning to challenge Roosevelt for the Republican presidential nomination in 1904. Within the Senate, four Republicans—Nelson W. Aldrich of Rhode Island, William B. Allison of Kansas, Orville H. Platt of Connecticut, and John C. Spooner of Wisconsin—had come to exercise a veto power over proposals brought before Congress. These

What: National politics
When: September 14, 1901
Where: Mainly Washington, D.C.
Who:
THEODORE ROOSEVELT (1858-1919), President of the United States from 1901 to 1909

men, known as the "oligarchs," expected to keep their special privileges during the Roosevelt presidency.

There were larger problems within the country. Industry had grown rapidly during the nineteenth century, and so had cities. Unjust labor practices and the problems of city life were placing new burdens on all levels of government. At the state and local levels, many reform-minded political leaders had come to power. They were demanding help from the federal government.

Meeting the Challenges

The president attacked his problems with skill and energy. Within the Republican Party, he was able to gain allies and undercut Senator Hanna's power. He made friends with the four Senate "oligarchs," so that they came to be his supporters rather than his enemies.

Roosevelt also identified himself with the reformers who were calling for changes in the practices of big industry. In March, 1902, he ordered the U.S. attorney general to file suit against the Northern Securities Company, one of the corporate giants of the railroad industry. Later that year, when an anthracite coal strike threat-

13

ened to leave city dwellers without fuel during the winter months, Roosevelt intervened personally to help resolve the dispute.

Actions such as these helped establish Roosevelt's political authority within the nation. Now he was able to give more attention to problems overseas. Because of his vision for the building of a canal that would link the Atlantic and Pacific oceans, he backed the actions of a revolutionary junta (group of leaders) that led Panama in seceding from Colombia. The way was cleared for the construction of the Panama Canal.

The Monroe Doctrine, formed by President James Monroe in the early 1800's, specified that the United States would resist European governments that tried to interfere in the affairs of independent nations of North and South America. Roosevelt now added what became known as the Roosevelt Corollary to the Monroe Doctrine: He claimed for the United States the right to exercise an international police power in Latin America in order to maintain the status quo and punish any government that did not conduct its affairs with decency. The Roosevelt Corollary was officially rejected by President Herbert Hoover in 1930, but to a large extent U.S. presidents have continued to follow its principles in dealing with Latin American states.

Roosevelt acted with similar decisiveness elsewhere in the world. In 1905, he took on the role of an arbitrator to help bring an end to the Russo-Japanese War. When his effort proved successful, he was awarded the Nobel Peace Prize.

Consequences

Early in Theodore Roosevelt's presidency, he showed great skill in dealing with powerful senators and with reform-minded politicians across the nation. He combined stubborn confidence with an ability to negotiate — qualities that served him well as he began to address international problems. Roosevelt was one of the first U.S. presidents to claim a prominent place for the United States — and for himself — in world affairs.

Roosevelt had a dramatic flair that captured the imagination of the American people. By focusing attention on his office and himself, he brought new power and prestige to the presidency and made the White House the focal point of American government.

Theodore Roosevelt. (*White House Historical Association*)

ANTHRACITE COAL MINERS STRIKE

> *Intervening to settle a coal miners' strike, President Theodore Roosevelt set a new precedent and increased the power of the United States presidency.*

What: Labor and national politics
When: May 12, 1902
Where: Pennsylvania and
    Washington, D.C.
Who:
THEODORE ROOSEVELT (1858-1919),
    President of the United States from
    1901 to 1909
JOHN MITCHELL (1870-1919), President
    of the United Mine Workers
GEORGE F. BAER (1842-1914), a mine
    operator and an owner of the
    Reading and Philadelphia Railroad
ELIHU ROOT (1845-1937), U.S.
    Secretary of War under Roosevelt
E. E. CLARK (1856-1930), Grand Chief
    of the Order of Railway Conductors
WILLIAM A. STONE (1846-1920),
    Governor of Pennsylvania

The Strike Is Launched

In 1902, anthracite coal miners were probably treated more unfairly than any other group of workers in the United States. They earned an average wage of $560 a year and had no guarantee of regular employment. Work in the mines was dangerous, and most of the miners lived in company-owned towns, so that their home life as well as their work was regulated by the mine owners.

United Mine Workers President John Mitchell served as a spokesman for these struggling workers. Threatening a strike in 1900, Mitchell

had won a 10 percent increase in their wages. Though further changes were desperately needed, in 1902 negotiations between owners and the union failed. On May 12, 147,000 members of the United Mine Workers walked out of the anthracite mines of Pennsylvania. Their demands included recognition of their union, a workday that would not exceed nine hours, more accurate weighing of the coal, and a 20 percent increase in pay.

At that time, it was not known that another readily available form of coal, bituminous, could be substituted for anthracite. As the strike dragged on toward winter, residents of northern cities began to fear that they would have to endure the cold months with no fuel to warm their houses. In September, the price of anthracite coal, usually five dollars a ton, reached fourteen dollars. Poor people, who bought in smaller quantities, paid a penny a pound, which added up to twenty dollars a ton.

By October, schools began to close, and the small stores of coal that were left sold for thirty and thirty-five dollars a ton. In the West, mobs began to seize coal cars from passing trains. Leaders in business feared that the whole country would break out in riots. Mayors across the nation appealed to the president for help.

The President Steps In

In response to their desperation, President Theodore Roosevelt arranged a conference between labor and management leaders at the White House on October 1, 1902. George F. Baer, the owner of the Reading and Philadelphia Railroad, represented the coal operators, while John Mitchell

Miners' wives search through a coal dump during the strike. (*Library of Congress*)

spoke for the striking miners. Many people across the country were already angry at Baer, for he had declared publicly that the rights of working men would be protected best "not by the labor agitators, but by the Christian men to whom God in his infinite wisdom has given the control of the property interests in this country." Baer was seen as proud and selfish, while Mitchell's manner was calm and polite.

The day-long conference between these two men failed, and it seemed that the strike could not be resolved peacefully. Mine owners claimed that the workers wanted to return to the mines but feared violence from the union. Yet, when Pennsylvania governor William A. Stone called out the state militia to protect anyone who wished to work, most of the miners remained on strike. Roosevelt began making a plan for federal troops

to occupy the mines, but at the same time Elihu Root, Secretary of War and a friend of the business community, worked to arrange a less drastic settlement.

On October 12, Root met with J. P. Morgan, a New York millionaire whose railroads crisscrossed the coal fields. Together they hammered out a possible compromise. The next day, George Baer was summoned to talk it over with Morgan, and by October 15, the mine operators had ratified the agreement. The Root-Morgan proposal was to establish a five-man independent commission that would be given authority to resolve the dispute. Presented with the proposal, the United Mine Workers insisted that a union representative and a Roman Catholic priest be appointed to the five-man panel. The mine operators agreed to the priest but stubbornly opposed inclusion of a union member.

Roosevelt himself broke the deadlock by naming E. E. Clark, Grand Chief of the Order of Railway Conductors, as a sixth member of the commission. In order to satisfy the mine operators, Roosevelt publicly labeled Clark "an eminent sociologist" rather than "a labor leader." The commission proceeded to find a compromise solution to the strike. The miners' union was not recognized, but the miners won a nine-hour day and a 10 percent pay raise. The weight dispute was settled, and a board of conciliation was created to help resolve future difficulties.

Consequences

President Theodore Roosevelt later spoke of the coal-strike settlement as a turning point in his administration. He was right. The settlement increased his personal popularity and added to the power of the U.S. presidency. Americans began to expect their presidents to be negotiators, able to help resolve both standoffs between business and labor, and serious conflicts elsewhere in the world.

THE UNITED STATES ACQUIRES THE PANAMA CANAL ZONE

In order to build a canal that would connect the Atlantic and Pacific oceans, the United States supported Panama's secession from Colombia and then purchased rights to a ten-mile "canal zone."

The Need for a Canal

Even in the time of Christopher Columbus and other early explorers of the New World, it was evident that a canal cutting through Central America would be very helpful to nations that engaged in world trade. For the United States, it became apparent during the Spanish-American War in 1898 that a canal would provide military advantages as well. To get from Puget Sound on the American West Coast to the Cuban war zone, the battleship *Oregon* had to journey all the way around Cape Horn, the southernmost tip of South America. The trip was so long that the *Oregon* almost missed the war.

The Clayton-Bulwer Treaty of 1850 between Great Britain and the United States, however, stipulated that neither nation could build a canal without the participation of the other. Yet Great Britain, eager to maintain its friendship with the United States, agreed to an all-American canal in 1900, in the first Hay-Paunceforte Treaty. The U.S. Senate refused to ratify this agreement, which specified that the canal would be neutral; the Senate insisted that the United States should have the right to defend the canal and keep a military presence there. An amendment to that effect was added, and Great Britain agreed reluctantly in the second Hay-Paunceforte Treaty of 1901.

Negotiations and Revolution

Yet the battle for a canal was only beginning. The major debate was over the route. Most members of Congress—and, in fact, most Ameri-

What: International relations and economics
When: November 18, 1903
Where: Washington, D.C.; Bogotá, Colombia; and Panama
Who:
THEODORE ROOSEVELT (1858-1919), President of the United States from 1901 to 1909
JOHN MILTON HAY (1838-1905), U.S. Secretary of State from 1898 to 1905
JOSÉ MANUEL MARROQUÍN (1827-1908), President of Colombia from 1900 to 1904
WILLIAM NELSON CROMWELL (1854-1948), a lawyer for the New Panama Canal Company
PHILIPPE JEAN BUNAU-VARILLA (1860-1940), a French engineer who became Minister of the Republic of Panama

cans—preferred a route that would go through Panama. President William McKinley's Isthmian Canal Commission supported this view, as did Senator John T. Morgan of the Senate Canals Committee. On January 9, 1902, the House approved a Nicaraguan route, and the Senate seemed ready to agree.

At this point, however, William Nelson Cromwell, lawyer for the New Canal Company, appeared on the scene. The New Canal Company had bought the assets and rights of the de Lesseps Company, which had proposed a canal through Panama but had gone out of business without building it. Cromwell was supported by Philippe Jean Bunau-Varilla, an engineer who was committed to constructing a canal through Panama. Cromwell offered the United States the rights to the Panamanian route for $40 million.

Cromwell was a skilled lobbyist, and the Panamanian route actually proved to have certain engineering advantages that would make a canal easier to build. Moreover, the proposed route through Nicaragua lay rather close to an erupting volcano. In view of these factors, President Theodore Roosevelt, the Canal Commission, and Congress all changed their minds. The result was the Spooner Act, which directed the president to build a canal through Panama if he could obtain the consent of Colombia, which owned Panama at

that time. If Colombia did not agree, the Nicaraguan route was to be chosen.

The nation of Colombia was racked by severe internal conflict at the turn of the century. A coup had just deposed the president, and Vice President José Manuel Marroquín had been elevated to the president's office. In this tense situation the United States began to put great pressure on Colombia to sign a canal treaty. John Milton Hay, U.S. Secretary of State, pushed through the Hay-Herrán Treaty, which was signed on January 22, 1903. Under this agreement, Colombia was to receive a onetime payment of $10 million and annual rents of $250,000, beginning in nine years, for rights to a canal zone six miles wide. The Colombian negotiators unwisely agreed not to ask for any of the $40 million being paid to the French canal company.

The treaty was quickly approved by the U.S.

Senate on March 17, 1903, and the American government settled back to wait for the expected approval by the Colombian legislature. President Roosevelt and members of the State Department failed, however, to understand the serious objections that the proud Colombians had to the treaty. Colombia was being asked to give up some of its sovereignty at a time when the United States was expanding its power worldwide. The treaty did not offer enough compensation for a route that had many engineering advantages and a profitable railroad. Furthermore, it did not take account of the fact that the French company's rights would expire in 1904 in any case, so that the United States would be freed from its obligation to pay the $40 million. With only three dissenting votes, the Colombian Senate rejected the treaty.

President Roosevelt reacted angrily to Colombia's decision and prepared to gain the canal zone by other means. According to State Department officials, an 1846 treaty between the United States and Colombia (then New Grenada) could be read to suggest that Americans had the right to guarantee the neutrality of and free passage through the Panamanian isthmus. The State Department and the president began to argue that the Colombian vote against the canal treaty was a denial of free passage.

There were those in Panama who had long wanted to separate from Colombia and, in fact, had been prevented when the United States came to Colombia's aid. Bunau-Varilla now led the way in encouraging a Panamanian revolution and kept Roosevelt informed of its progress. Claiming to be guaranteeing free transit in the isthmus, Roo-sevelt sent the cruiser *Nashville* to the scene.

Panama City, on the Pacific side of the country, was taken by the revolutionaries on November 2, 1903. On the Atlantic side, the *Nashville* landed American forces at Colón to keep Colombian troops from passing across the isthmus and defeating the rebels. Bunau-Varilla bribed the Colombian general to leave Colón, and the revolution had succeeded without lives being taken.

On November 18, 1903, Panama's new minister, Bunau-Varilla, joined Secretary Hay in signing the Hay-Bunau-Varilla Treaty. The United States agreed to pay $10 million cash and an annual rent of $250,000 in return for a canal zone ten miles wide that was to remain under permanent American control.

Consequences

The Americans took possession of the canal site on May 4, 1904, and built the canal at a cost of more than $300 million. The Panama Canal was opened for shipping on August 15, 1914, two weeks after World War I began in Europe. Throughout the twentieth century the canal was extremely important for international shipping and as a U.S. military outpost.

The United States continued to operate the canal under the 1903 treaty provisions until the 1960's, when growing Panamanian nationalism led to pressure for the canal's return to Panamanian control. Throughout Latin America, the canal had become a symbol for North American "imperialism" — the United States' apparent readiness to ignore the rights of other nations in order to enrich itself.

Panamanian soldiers guard a village en route from Colombia. (*Library of Congress*)

RUSSIA AND JAPAN BATTLE OVER TERRITORY

> *The conflicting imperial ambitions of Russia and Japan led to a war over domination of Manchuria and Korea.*

What: Military conflict
When: February 9, 1904-September 5, 1905
Where: Manchuria, Korea, and the Yellow Sea
Who:
NICHOLAS II (1868-1918), Czar of Russia from 1894 to 1917
SERGEI YULIEVICH WITTE (1849-1915), Russian Minister of Finance from 1892 to 1903
ADMIRAL EVGENI IVANOVICH ALEKSEEV (1843-1918), commander of the Russian fleet in the Far East from 1904 to 1905
GENERAL ALEKSEI NIKOLAEVICH KURO-PATKIN (1848-1921), Russian Minister of War and Supreme Commander of Russian forces in the Far East from 1904 to 1905
ADMIRAL ZINOVI PETROVICH ROZHDEST-VENSKI (1848-1909), commander of the Russian Baltic fleet
WILLIAM II (1859-1941), Emperor of Germany from 1888 to 1918
THEODORE ROOSEVELT (1858-1919), President of the United States from 1901 to 1909
ADMIRAL TŌGŌ HEIHACHIRŌ (1848-1934), commander of the Japanese Baltic fleet

War Begins

Influenced by the Western nations' drive to expand their control over other territories, both Russia and Japan had, by the end of the nineteenth century, become imperialist powers themselves in the Far East. When both of them attempted to expand their holdings in Manchuria and Korea, they came into conflict.

Between 1901 and 1904, Japanese and Russian officials negotiated to try to agree on the exact limits of their countries' control in these regions. Among the Russians, however, there were two distinct groups that made negotiations between the two countries difficult. Count Sergei Yulievich Witte, Minister of Finance, and Count Vladimir Nikolaevich Lamsdorff, Minister of Foreign Affairs, joined General Aleksei Nikolaevich Kuropatkin, Minister of War, in favoring accommodation with Japan.

The other group, led by Aleksandr Bezobrazov, persuaded Czar Nicholas II that the Russians needed to respond to Japan with a policy of military strength.

In 1903, there was an increase in revolutionary activity in Russia. In times of war, feelings of patriotism tend to increase. Russian government officials thought that if Russia were threatened by a foreign foe, the Russian people would rally around the government, and revolution would become less attractive.

Meanwhile, the Japanese shored up their position by making an alliance with Great Britain, a traditional foe of Russia, in 1902. With increased confidence, the Japanese representatives became just as stubborn as the Russians during the 1903 negotiations. The talks between Russia and Japan reached a deadlock in early 1904.

Soldiers of the Russian Empire pass through the gates of Mukden, Manchuria. (*Library of Congress*)

On February 9, 1904, the Japanese mounted a surprise attack on the Russian fleet at Port Arthur, in the Yellow Sea, and decimated it. Russian national pride was dealt a major blow; after all, Russia was a huge country, while Japan was tiny. As the Russians scrambled to respond to the attack, Japanese troops were able to disembark on the mainland without opposition.

Because the Trans-Siberian Railway had not been completed, Russian reinforcements were slow to arrive, and the Japanese forces defeated Russian armies in Manchuria. In a series of major battles along the Yalu River on the border between Korea and Manchuria, and at Liaoyang and Mukden in Manchuria itself, the Japanese defeated Russia again and again. A standoff was finally reached near Mukden in October, 1904.

Meanwhile, the Russian government tried desperately to balance Japan's naval forces by sending its Baltic Fleet, commanded by Admiral Zinovi Petrovich Rozhdestvenski, to the Far East. This fleet finally arrived in the China Sea after nar-

rowly avoiding a conflict with Great Britain, but by then Port Arthur had surrendered. Rozhdestvenski set sail for Vladivostok. On May 24, 1905, the Baltic Fleet was waylaid by a Japanese flotilla in the Tsushima Straits, between Korea and Japan. By the end of the battle, the Russian fleet had been practically annihilated.

Peace Negotiations

Such major defeats on land and sea, made worse by the revolutionary activity within Russia, made Nicholas II grateful to accept the help of American President Theodore Roosevelt and German Emperor William II. They arranged for peace negotiations to be held in Portsmouth, New Hampshire.

By the time of the negotiations, though Japan had been winning the war, its resources were seriously depleted. Witte, who represented Russia at the peace conference, was able to take advantage of this situation, so that Russia did not suffer heavy losses under the terms of the agreement. By a treaty signed on September 5, 1905,

Russia surrendered to Japan the areas already lost during the fighting. Japan was to keep control of the Liaotung Peninsula, the naval base of Port Arthur, and Dalny, a commercial port. Russia also surrendered control over the South Manchurian Railway, and the southern portion of the island of Sakhalin was transferred to Japan.

Consequences

The Russo-Japanese War had repercussions around the world. Russia had lost some of its influence in the southern European Balkan States, and Germany would move in to fill the gap. France began to lose confidence in Russia, while Great Britain and Russia began to let go of their old rivalry in Asia.

Within Russia, the war and defeat added fuel to the revolutionary movement, which would eventually culminate in the 1917-1918 Bolshevik Revolution. In Japan, the terms of peace, which were seen as too soft on Russia, brought about a mood of frustration among the people and the leaders, and a spirit of nationalism began to arise.

BRITAIN AND FRANCE FORM THE ENTENTE CORDIALE

> *Realizing that both countries had much to gain by leaving behind their old rivalry, leaders of France and Great Britain entered into a new relationship of cooperation.*

Need for Good Relations

As colonial powers, Great Britain and France had been rivals through the eighteenth and nineteenth centuries. As the twentieth century began, however, leaders of both countries began to realize that much could be gained through a new friendship between them.

There were several reasons that better relations were needed. In the Far East, tension was growing between Japan (an ally of Great Britain) and Russia (an ally of France). In 1904, the Russo-Japanese War broke out, and if Great Britain and France were to avoid being drawn into war against each other, they needed to mend their hostile relations.

The 1898 Fashoda crisis, a struggle for control of Sudan, had already brought France and Great Britain into conflict in Africa. More conflict over African colonies seemed possible. For more than a quarter century, France had claimed certain political and financial rights in Egypt, a region Great Britain was attempting to control. At the same time, France wanted control of Morocco. Groups of Moroccans often carried out raids against French settlements in neighboring Algeria; if France could dominate Morocco, then, it would be in a much better position to protect its other North African holdings. Great Britain's large share of Morocco's trade, however, was an obstacle to France's aims. Great Britain and France also continued to dispute rights to fisheries in Newfoundland.

Within Europe, Great Britain made numerous attempts between 1898 and 1901 to enter into an alliance with Germany. Yet the Boer War of

What: International relations
When: April 8, 1904
Where: London and Paris
Who:
SIR THOMAS BARCLAY (1853-1941), a British official active in international relations
HENRY CHARLES KEITH PETTY-FITZMAURICE, MARQUIS OF LANSDOWNE (1845-1927), Foreign Secretary of Great Britain from 1900 to 1905
EDWARD VII (1841-1910), King of Great Britain from 1901 to 1910
THÉOPHILE DELCASSÉ (1852-1923), French Minister of Foreign Affairs from 1898 to 1906
ÉMILE LOUBET (1838-1929), President of France from 1899 to 1906
PIERRE-PAUL CAMBON (1848-1924), French ambassador at London

1899-1902 increased anti-British feeling in Germany. With Germany refusing to come into alliance, and with the buildup of the German navy, which began to threaten British domination of the seas, British leaders looked increasingly to France. At the same time, France had been disappointed by its alliance with Russia, which had been financially costly and had not brought much reward to the French.

Steps Toward Friendship

Both the British and the French governments

25

appointed new officials to improve relations between their countries. The new Minister of Foreign Affairs in France, Théophile Delcassé, tried to persuade the British to agree to France's domination over Morocco. In return, he was willing to avoid a confrontation with British forces at Fashoda in 1898. On March 21, 1899, he reached an agreement with Great Britain about how the two colonial powers would divide their influence in the Upper Nile (Egypt) and the Congo.

A year later, Sir Thomas Barclay and Delcassé cooperated to bring British chambers of commerce to visit the great Paris Exposition. Barclay also arranged a return visit of French chambers of commerce to England.

On October 14, 1903, both states signed the Anglo-French Treaty of Arbitration, promising to submit most of their disputes to the Permanent Court of Arbitration at The Hague, in the Netherlands. Barclay was quite involved in negotiating this treaty, and he also helped bring about an exchange of visits between King Edward VII and President Émile Loubet in 1903.

When Loubet went to London, Delcassé accompanied him and took the opportunity to begin serious discussions with Henry Charles Keith Petty-Fitzmaurice — Marquis of Lansdowne and British Foreign Secretary — to settle the conflicts that remained between Great Britain and France. The result was that on April 8, 1904, Lansdowne and French Ambassador Pierre-Paul Cambon signed the Entente Cordiale.

The Entente Cordiale was not a military pact, but it resolved a number of disputes having to do with the Newfoundland fisheries, West African boundaries, Siam, Madagascar, and the New Hebrides Islands. Most important, France agreed to allow Great Britain a free hand in Egypt in exchange for being allowed a free hand in Morocco. A secret provision of the Entente Cordiale was that Morocco would eventually be divided between Spain and France: Spain would control

the coastal area, opposite Gibraltar, while the French occupied the inland area.

Consequences

Delcassé and other French leaders were pleased to have gained greater control over Morocco. Germany, however, also had interests in Morocco, and German leaders, especially those in the Foreign Office, were insulted that Delcassé apparently thought he could disregard them.

Since France was already allied with Russia, the balance of power in Europe was beginning to make the Germans uneasy. Germany attempted to defend its Moroccan interests in 1905 and 1911, and two serious crises resulted. The effect was to strengthen bonds between Great Britain and France even further, and to push Germany further away. The overall effect was to divide Europe into two armed camps, which would move against each other in 1914 and set off World War I.

King's carriage leaving Longchamps with Loubet and King Edward in May, 1903. (*Library of Congress*)

RUSSIAN WORKERS AND CZARIST TROOPS CLASH ON BLOODY SUNDAY

> *A peaceful demonstration by workers in Saint Petersburg ended when czarist troops killed about one hundred protesters.*

What: Civil strife
When: January 22, 1905
Where: Saint Petersburg, Russia
Who:
NICHOLAS II (1868-1918), Czar of Russia from 1894 to 1917
FATHER GEORGI APPOLLONOVICH GAPON (1870-1906), a Russian Orthodox priest

Rising Discontent

A severe economic depression from 1900 to 1902 made life for Russian peasants and city workers even more difficult than it had been. Between 1900 and 1905, unemployment increased in large centers of industry such as Moscow and Saint Petersburg. Workers went on strike over low wages and long hours.

Many Russians were angry about their government's seeming indifference to their poverty. Czar Nicholas II and a number of his closest advisers, including Konstantin Petrovich Pobedonostsev, Procurator of the Holy Synod, were seen as stubbornly conservative and resistant to changes that might benefit the common people of Russia. Faced with the need for social and political reform, and frustrated at the government's inaction, various revolutionary reformers were driven to desperate acts.

Unrest in the cities spread to the countryside, where peasants began to revolt with the encouragement of the Social Revolutionary Party. In the cities, the workers were supported by the Social Democrats and an organization—known as the Society for the Mutual Help of the Workers in the Engineering Industry—founded in Moscow in 1902 by Sergei Zubatov, head of the city's security police. This movement actually received some support from the government, for it was designed to make sure that the workers would not adopt a program of political reform. This movement of "police socialism" was mostly staffed by police officials. It soon collapsed in Moscow but reappeared in Saint Petersburg under the leadership of a Russian Orthodox priest, Father Georgi Appollonovich Gapon.

Father Gapon's organization also received government recognition as being nonpolitical. Actually, it was nonpolitical at first, but by 1904, when its membership had grown to eight thousand, many of its members were attracted to the more revolutionary socialist approach of the Social Democrats and Social Revolutionaries. Laborers were becoming more and more disgusted with their working conditions. Russia's war losses to Japan, such as the fall of Port Arthur in December, 1904, were another reason for discontent among the Russian people.

Petition and Protest

In January, 1905, a large factory in the capital dismissed many workers. Fellow workers began a protest strike, which within a few days had spread across the city. Gapon's organization met on January 20, 1905, and its members angrily decided that he should lead a march to the Czar's Winter

28

Palace in Saint Petersburg and present Nicholas II with a petition.

The workers and the radical intellectuals who helped to draft the petition reaffirmed their loyalty to the czar. Yet the petition called on him to lift from their shoulders the yoke of oppression that his corrupt officials had placed on them. The petitioners demanded better treatment from officials and factory owners, and an end to the war with Japan. They also asked for major civil and political reforms, including freedom of speech, freedom of the press, and freedom of association; broader voting rights for local elections; equality under the law; and, above all, the creation of a representative assembly to make laws for the country.

For Russia at that time in its history, these demands were truly revolutionary. Father Gapon believed that some of the petition's demands went too far, but the bitterly cold Sunday morning of January 22, 1905, found him leading his followers to the Czar's Winter Palace.

Wearing his priestly robes, Father Gapon led long columns of workers from the outskirts of Saint Petersburg toward the center of the city and the Winter Palace. The march was intended as a peaceful demonstration, and some marchers were accompanied by their families. Others carried religious images and portraits of the czar. Nevertheless, if the czar rejected the petition, the marchers were prepared to use force to achieve their demands. Gapon had assured them that part of the army would side with them and provide them with arms if fighting was necessary.

Police spies within Gapon's organization, however, had alerted the government to have military forces prepared for action. When the workers approached the Winter Palace and refused to break up their demonstration, the army troops, who remained loyal to the czar, fired on them. About a hundred workers were killed, and Gapon was unable to deliver the petition. The workers had not realized that Nicholas had left the city a few days earlier.

Consequences

The march and massacre of January 22, 1905, came to be known as "Bloody Sunday." This tragic episode triggered the first Russian revolution in the twentieth century. Father Gapon managed to escape from the capital and fled into exile. From his place of exile he issued an open letter to the czar, denouncing him for having refused to accept the petition. "Let all blood which has to be shed fall upon thee, hangman, and thy kindred." In this statement, Gapon expressed the real historical consequence of Bloody Sunday: The Russian people had now completely lost faith in the czar. The massacre made it clear to all that the Russian autocratic government was bent on protecting itself, not the Russian people.

Gapon's appeal for revolution was soon answered by strikes of workers throughout Russia. Although the Revolution of 1905 lasted less than a year and did not succeed in its aims, Nicholas II never felt secure afterward. His failure to respond to the needs of workers had led to the revolution, and the disasters Russia suffered in the war with Japan had added fuel to the flames. Yet an even greater disaster, World War I, was soon to come; it provided the occasion in 1917 for a successful revolution that finally toppled czarist autocracy in Russia.

> *Norway dissolved its union with Sweden and became completely independent for the first time since 1380.*

Desire for Independence

In 1380, Norway had entered into a union with Denmark that brought the two countries under one ruler; this union lasted until 1814. After the Vienna Settlement ending the Napoleonic Wars, Finland was taken from Sweden and given to Russia. In return, Russia's czar, Alexander I, promised to support Sweden's annexation of Norway. By Sweden and Denmark's Treaty of Kiel in 1814, Norway was annexed to Sweden.

Yet the Norwegian people remained stubbornly independent. On May 17, 1814, a Norwegian assembly adopted a liberal constitution that provided for a parliament, the Storting, and severely restricted the rights of the executive branch of government, represented by a monarch. The constituent assembly then proceeded to elect a Danish prince as king.

In response, Sweden invaded Norway, which then had to submit to Swedish rule. Yet on November 4, 1814, the Storting declared Norway to be "a free, independent, and indivisible kingdom, united with Sweden under one king." In 1815 Sweden accepted this declaration and set up a special agreement, the Riksakt, to define the relationship between the two countries. The Riksakt was not a very clear or consistent agreement; for example, it gave the Swedish government authority to conduct foreign affairs for both countries, but the consular service was a shared responsibility.

Norway and Sweden were very different in the makeup of their populations and in their traditions of government. Norway was made up mostly of free peasants and people who made their living

What: Political independence
When: October 26, 1905
Where: Norway and Sweden
Who:
OSCAR II (1829-1907), King of Sweden from 1872 to 1907, and King of Norway from 1872 to 1905
JOHAN SVERDRUP (1816-1892), Norwegian Liberal leader, President from the Storting from 1871 to 1881
ERIK GUSTAF BOSTRÖM (1842-1907), Prime Minister of Sweden in 1904
PETER CHRISTIAN MICHELSEN (1857-1925), Norwegian Radical leader, Premier of Norway from 1905 to 1907
HAAKON VII (1872-1957), King of Norway from 1905 to 1957 (formerly Prince Carl of Denmark)

from the sea, while in Sweden, there was an aristocracy that owned most of the land and kept the peasants dependent. By the mid-1800's, Sweden had developed considerable industry, but Norway remained primarily agricultural and commercial. Norway's liberal structure of government was quite different from Sweden's conservative system, which was run by the aristocracy.

A rising nationalism in Norway was fostered by a great interest in Norwegian language and folklore. Late in the nineteenth century, playwright Henrik Ibsen and writer Björnstjerne Björnson led a Norwegian literary revival. Young Norwegians became passionately committed to breaking off their country's union with Sweden. The Liberal Party emerged after 1870 as the champion of Norwegian democracy and greater freedom for Norway within the union. By 1890, however, the Radical Party had attracted many young nationalists with its call for a complete breaking of the union with Sweden.

Steps Toward Separation

The Norwegian Liberal leader Johan Sverdrup issued a call for changing the terms of union to permit members of the Norwegian ministry, who were appointed by the Crown, to take part in the deliberations of the Storting. The Storting passed resolutions to this effect three times, but each time King Oscar II exercised his veto. In June,

1880, the Storting passed still another resolution making Sverdrup's proposal a part of the constitution. Because the Liberals had just won a major victory at the polls, the king finally had to accept the amendment. This marked the full establishment of parliamentary government in Norway.

Under the Military Service Act, supported by Radicals and passed by the Storting in 1885, Norway withdrew the largest and best part of its military forces from the common army of the union. This caused a further weakening of the monarchy and of the union.

In 1891, the Radicals won a majority of votes and took control of the ministry and the Storting. They then raised the issue that led to the end of the union between Sweden and Denmark. Contrary to

the provisions of the Riksakt, they demanded a separate Norwegian consular service. On this matter the Radicals came up against the opposition of both the Swedish government and the Norwegian Conservative Party. These two groups agreed to try to resolve not only this question but also all other matters that had been sources of tension between the two nations. So it was that Sweden began what proved to be a long series of negotiations leading nowhere.

At first, the Swedes insisted on keeping a joint consular service but proposed giving Norway an equal share in the conduct of foreign policy. This proposal failed. In 1902, Sweden reopened negotiations and agreed to the Radical demand for separate consular services. The Radical government was defeated in 1903, and it seemed that the negotiations had a chance of success. Yet in 1904, the very stubborn, uncompromising Erik Gustaf Boström became Prime Minister of Sweden and began to insist that Norway's consular service could not be allowed real independence from Sweden's Foreign Ministry. On February 7, 1905, the two governments announced that negotiations were formally over.

Ironically, Boström had managed to unite the people of Norway as never before against Sweden. In March, 1905, the Radicals returned to power in Norway under the leadership of Peter Christian Michelsen. Along with the Radical-dominated Storting, Michelsen moved to destroy the union. In May, 1905, the Storting passed a bill calling for the establishment of a separate Norwegian consular service. When the king vetoed the bill, the entire Norwegian ministry resigned. Oscar refused to accept the resignations, and on June 7 the Storting declared that the royal power had ceased to function.

Consequences

In a vote on August 13, 1905, the Norwegian people approved ending the union with Sweden by the overwhelming majority of 368,208 to 184. The Swedish parliament reluctantly accepted the separation on September 24. A month later, on October 26, the two states signed a formal treaty dissolving the union. Norway then bestowed the crown on Prince Carl of Denmark (grandson of King Christian IX of Denmark), who ruled until 1957 as Haakon VII.

Schoolchildren of Odde celebrate Independence Day, 1906. (*Library of Congress*)

The October Manifesto Promises Constitutional Government in Russia

Though Nicholas II's October Manifesto promised important freedoms under the guarantee of a new constitution, his later actions fell far short of his promises.

What: National politics
When: October 30, 1905
Where: Saint Petersburg, Russia
Who:
Nicholas II (1868-1918), Czar of Russia from 1894 to 1917
Count Sergei Yulievich Witte (1849-1915), first constitutional Premier of Russia, from 1905 to 1906
Alexander Dubrovin (1855-1918), President of the Union of the Russian People, a reactionary group
Leon Trotsky (1879-1940), leader of the leftist Soviet of Workers' Deputies

Constitutional Manifesto

Growing discontent among Russian workers and peasants had led to a public call for government reform in January, 1905, in Saint Petersburg. Czarist troops had opened fire on the demonstrators, initiating a massacre that had come to be known as Bloody Sunday. This episode combined with Russia's losses in the Russo-Japanese War of 1904-1905 to touch off the Revolution of 1905.

Between January and October, 1905, there were strikes in industrial cities and peasant revolts in the countryside, along with mutinies in the army and navy. Seeking to calm the people, Czar

Nicholas II proclaimed in August the establishment of the Duma, or Russian parliament. He did not propose giving the Duma much power: It would be elected only indirectly, and the vote would be given only to a few. Furthermore, it would not have power to make laws, only to advise the czar.

His proclamation did not have the effect he had hoped. In October, a general strike brought almost all activity in the country to a standstill for ten days. The pressure on Nicholas had increased. Count Sergei Yulievich Witte, his former finance minister and now premier, drafted a constitution, which Nicholas reluctantly agreed to publish as an imperial manifesto.

If fully carried out, the October Manifesto would have given Russia a constitutional monarchy. It had several important provisions to liberalize the government. The manifesto guaranteed civil liberties such as freedom of speech, assembly, and conscience; freedom of the press; freedom from arbitrary arrest; and the right to form trade unions. Citizens who had been excluded from voting under the August decree would receive the right to vote. The manifesto promised that no law would be enacted without the consent of the Duma, and it gave the Duma the right to decide whether actions of the czar's officials were legal.

The People Respond

Government officials had hoped that publication of the October Manifesto would quiet the country. Instead, the Russian people responded

Holiday crowd in Moscow celebrates the declaration of liberty by the czar. (*Library of Congress*)

with more disorder. Those who supported the manifesto demonstrated against those who opposed the new freedoms. The revolutionary movement split between rejecters and supporters of the new constitution. In the end, this worked in the government's favor.

On the extreme Right, conservatives who were loyal to the government and the Russian Orthodox Church organized the Union of the Russian People under the presidency of Alexander Dubrovin. Czar Nicholas himself belonged to this group. Some of these conservatives led the Black Hundreds — gangs of tough young men — in demonstrations supporting the czar. During the week after the manifesto's publication, the Black Hundreds launched many attacks on Jewish people, many of whom lost property or were killed.

The Octobrists were moderate Rightists who were very pleased with the October Manifesto and called it the climax of a successful revolution. The Constitutional Democrats, also known as Cadets, also favored the manifesto but urged the government to move quickly on land reform and other issues.

Leftist parties rejected the manifesto completely, insisting that it did not do enough for the Russian people. They attempted to continue the revolution. The Soviet (Council) of Workers' Deputies in Saint Petersburg, made up of members of the Social Revolutionary, Bolshevik, and Menshevik parties, had been set up before the manifesto was published. Now its leaders, including Leon Trotsky, laid plans for new strikes, which they hoped would lead to an armed uprising.

Though peasant revolts and mutinies in the armed forces continued, the Soviet of Workers' Deputies began to lose the support of urban workers. The program of strikes did not succeed, and by mid-December the government had arrested the leaders. In Moscow the Soviet of Workers' Deputies took up arms against the czar, but by the end of the month the government was able to defeat them.

Consequences

The Revolution of 1905 did not succeed; the czarist monarchy had survived. Nicholas II had lost some of his confidence, but he now began to take back his traditional autocratic way of ruling the nation. The October Manifesto had served its purpose, gaining some support for Nicholas among the people and dividing the revolutionary movement. Its provisions were not put into practice.

Though historians speak of the Revolution of 1905 in Russia, the uprisings of that year were actually only a revolt that prepared the way for the Revolution of 1917. At the end of 1905, the czar remained on the throne, most of the army remained loyal, and the promises of the October Manifesto had proved hollow. Yet the people's discontent had not been squelched, and it would rise again to end czarist rule for good in 1917.

THE FIRST RUSSIAN DUMA CONVENES

The new Russian parliament, established by Czar Nicholas II in an attempt to quiet those who criticized his domineering way of governing the country, was not given a chance to exercise any real authority.

Limits Set for the Duma

In August, 1905, as workers' and peasants' revolts were breaking out across Russia, Czar Nicholas II issued a proclamation that a Duma, or parliament, would be established for the country. In October, he followed that announcement with a draft constitution called the October Manifesto. Before the end of the year, there were further uprisings in Saint Petersburg, Moscow, and elsewhere, but the czar and his army were able to suppress them.

As 1906 began, there was continued debate in Russia over whether a constitutional monarchy should be established or whether the absolute monarchy of the czar should be continued and strengthened. Politicians prepared for the elections to the first Duma. The election laws, drawn up by Count Sergei Witte, allowed for indirect election of representatives. The majority of the representatives would be assigned to rural landowners and peasants, for the czar believed that these people would be less likely to press for political reform than would townspeople and industrial workers.

The czar and his ministers tried to put strict limits on the power of the Duma. For example, the czar made the state council an upper legislative chamber—parallel to Great Britain's House of Lords or to the U.S. Senate—that would have powers equal to those of the Duma. Half the members of this upper chamber were appointed directly by the czar, and the other half were elected by traditionally conservative groups such as the clergy, provincial assemblies, the aristo-

What: National politics
When: May 10, 1906
Where: Saint Petersburg, Russia
Who:
Nicholas II (1868-1918), Czar of Russia from 1894 to 1917
Count Sergei Yulievich Witte (1849- 1915), first constitutional Premier of Russia, from November, 1905, to May, 1906
Paul Miliukov (1859- 1943), leader of the Constitutional Democrats, or Cadets
Aleksandr Ivanovich Guchkov (1862-1936), leader of the Octobrists
Ivan Loginovich Goremykin (1839-1917), Premier of Russia from May to July, 1906
Pëtr Arkadevich Stolypin (1862-1911), Premier of Russia in July, 1906

crats, and managers of businesses.

The week before the Duma's first meeting, the government issued a set of "fundamental laws" specifying what powers the Duma would *not* have. No bills were to become law until they were passed by both houses and signed by the czar. The czar's ministers were responsible to him alone, not to the Duma. The Duma did not have complete control of the budget: If the two houses approved different budget figures, the czar could accept either set, and if no budget was passed by the Duma, the government could continue to use the one adopted the previous year. The czar would keep absolute control over foreign policy, appointments, censorship, the armed forces, the police, and the summoning and dismissal of the Duma. When the Duma was not in session, the czar could rule by decree.

The result of the election laws, the creation of an upper house composed of the state council, and the "fundamental laws" was that the political reforms promised by the October Manifesto could not possibly come about.

Election and Convening

The two leading political parties, which could both be described as moderate, were the Constitutional Democratic Party, or Cadets, and the Union of October 17, or Octobrists. Both of these parties had come into existence only the previous year, but they competed vigorously against each other in the election campaigns. For the most part, the radical Social Revolutionaries and the Social Democrats boycotted the election.

The Cadets, led by a respected Russian historian named Paul Miliukov, urged that a parliamentary government with a constitutional monarchy be established. The Duma should be fully involved in writing a new constitution, the Cadets said, and there should be a program of land reform to buy huge rural estates from the owners and put land under the control of the common people. The Octobrists, whose leader was Aleksandr Ivanovich Guchkov, had a more conservative platform; they especially disagreed with the Cadets' land-reform proposal.

When the votes were counted, the Cadets had won 180 of the Duma's 520 seats, while the Octobrists won only 12. In all, some forty political groups made up the first Duma.

With a speech from the throne, Nicholas II

formally convened the Duma's first meeting on May 10, 1906, in the Winter Palace in Saint Petersburg. From the beginning, it was obvious that the government had no intention of allowing the Duma to exercise any real power. The czar's officials had been alarmed to see that conservative groups had failed to elect a single representative to the Duma. Still, the czar expected the Duma to be fairly conservative in its dealings. He was quite surprised when, shortly after its convocation, the Duma presented an "address to the throne" in which it demanded a universal right to vote, direct elections, abolition of the upper chamber, parliamentary government, and land reform.

Witte resigned as premier, and Ivan Goremykin took his place. On May 26, Goremykin addressed the Duma and rejected all its demands. Undaunted, the Duma continued to call for extensive political reforms over the next two months. During this time, Nicholas considered a proposal to bring Cadets into the government in order to silence the Duma's criticism. Yet Miliukov was reluctant to accept such a compromise, as was Pëtr Stolypin, the czar's Minister of the Interior. Finally, Nicholas simply dissolved the Duma on July 21. On that same day Stolypin was appointed to succeed Goremykin as premier. He was a hard-liner who became known for his conservative policies.

Consequences

About two hundred Duma deputies refused to accept the closing down of the Duma. Crossing the border into the Grand Duchy of Finland, they gathered in the town of Viborg and signed the "Viborg Manifesto," written by Paul Miliukov. In this appeal, the deputies said that the government's closing of the Duma was illegal. They also insisted that the government could not collect taxes or draft men for military service without the Duma's consent.

The men who signed this appeal were sentenced to three months in prison. As a result, they were considered criminals and were not eligible to run for reelection to the next Duma, which was scheduled to meet early in 1907. Having been deprived of some of its best political leaders, the drive for a constitutional form of government in Russia lost much of its force in the years before the outbreak of the Revolution of 1917.

The first Duma in session. (*Library of Congress*)

THE *DREADNOUGHT* REVOLUTIONIZES NAVAL ARCHITECTURE

The design of a new, heavier, and faster battleship allowed Great Britain to retain its naval superiority in the early twentieth century.

What: Military technology
When: December, 1906
Where: Portsmouth, England
Who:
ADMIRAL SIR JOHN ARBUTHNOT FISHER (1841-1920), First Sea Lord at the British Admiralty from 1904 to 1910
REAR ADMIRAL PRINCE LOUIS ALEXANDER OF BATTENBERG (1854-1921), British Director of Naval Intelligence from 1902 to 1905
SIR PHILIP WATTS (1846-1926), Director of the Construction of the Royal Navy from 1902 to 1912

New Armaments

In 1900, battleships were armed with guns of different calibers, and normally their ranges did not extend beyond three thousand yards. British warships of the *King Edward VII* class, designed in 1901, carried four 12-inch guns, ten 6-inch guns, four 9.2-inch guns, and a battery of small guns for defense against torpedo boats. These ships weighed 16,350 tons and could steam at 18.5 knots.

New developments in naval armaments raised new problems in the design of battleships. First, the accuracy and range of torpedoes were more than doubled, from about three thousand yards to seven thousand yards or more. As a result, opposing formations of battleships would need to keep a greater distance from each other, so that they would have a better chance of avoiding these very dangerous weapons.

Second, telescopic sights and new electrical fire-control equipment allowed accurate gunfire to be delivered at a range of eight thousand or more yards. At such a great distance, though, it was difficult, perhaps even impossible, to tell the difference between the splashes of shells from different calibers of guns — and so it was hard to correct their aim.

With improved weapons to fire farther and more accurately, a new type of battleship was needed.

Design and Construction

In 1900 Admiral Sir John Arbuthnot Fisher, who was then commander-in-chief of the Royal Navy's Mediterranean station, came up with the idea of a ship that would carry only big guns. With no medium-sized guns, there would be no need to figure out which splashes were caused by which shells. The ship would carry a larger number of heavy guns than older ships did, along with some light, quick-fire artillery to be used against torpedo craft.

When Fisher became First Sea Lord at the Admiralty in October, 1904, he had the chance to try out his new ideas. With technical help from W. H. Gard, chief naval constructor at Portsmouth Dockyard, he had several sketch plans drawn up and submitted to a special Committee on Design. The committee included Rear Admiral Prince Louis Alexander of Battenberg, who as Director of Naval Intelligence had information on battleship designs that were being developed in other countries. Other committee members were

HMS *Dreadnought.* (*Library of Congress*)

Sir Philip Watts, the Royal Navy's Director of Construction; six expert officers of high rank; and six naval architects who were civilians. The committee chose one design from those that had been submitted, and they appointed J. H. Narbeth, a naval constructor, to make the final working drawings. In March, 1905, his plans were accepted.

The final design was for a ship of 17,900 tons armed with ten 12-inch guns mounted in twin turrets, three on the center line, and one on each side forward. Eight guns would point out from each side of the ship, and six could point ahead or astern. No medium artillery would be included, but there would be an antidestroyer battery of twenty-seven rapid-firing 12-pound guns. Armor eleven inches thick would protect the body of the ship, and its powerful turbine engines — the first ever fitted in a battleship — would bring it to a speed of twenty-one knots. This ship would be able to overwhelm any existing battleship with superior fire, and its speed guaranteed that it could run down any weaker ship or escape from a large group of enemy ships. The new vessel was to be named H.M.S. *Dreadnought*.

The turbine engines were an extremely important part of the *Dreadnought*'s design. Previous battleships had been powered by reciprocating steam engines. In the *Dreadnought*, turbines weighing no more than the older reciprocating

steam engines would provide more horsepower, would give more speed, would use up less fuel at high speeds, and, having fewer moving parts, would be easier to maintain.

The materials needed for the ship's construction were collected quickly. The 12-inch guns and mountings that had been intended for two other ships then being built, the *Lord Nelson* and the *Agamemnon*, were taken for use in the *Dreadnought*. Every effort was made to complete the new battleship rapidly. In great secrecy, the *Dreadnought*'s keel was laid at Portsmouth on October 2, 1905.

With great fanfare, the ship was launched on February 10, 1906. By October 3, it was structurally complete — only a year and a day from its beginning. At once it was headed out to sea for tests. Some who were involved in the *Dreadnought*'s design and construction feared that the shock of firing eight guns at once might damage the ship's hull. That problem did not arise, however, and the ship performed well in its trials. After a few minor adjustments, the *Dreadnought* was formally placed in service in December, 1906.

Consequences

The successful completion of this new type of battleship had important effects for the naval construction of all the Great Powers. The first announcement of the *Dreadnought*'s successful trials was the same as saying that all the battleships of the world were now obsolete. As a result, most countries stopped constructing battleships while they assigned their designers to make plans for more modern ships.

Germany did not produce its version of a new battleship until July, 1907. By that time Great Britain already had the *Dreadnought* in commission, and since its design was clearly successful, three similar ships of the *Bellerophon* class were constructed in 1907.

Until this time, Great Britain's fleet of battleships had been twice as large as Germany's. In creating a ship that made the rest of its fleet obsolete, the British were in one sense giving Germany the chance to catch up. Yet if the British Navy had not acted when it did, and Germany, Japan, and the United States had suddenly decided to build their own superior battleships, Great Britain would have found itself in the more difficult position of needing to catch up.

As Germany and Great Britain began their battleship-building race, the British pulled ahead. Between 1910 and 1912 the two nations held conferences to try to set limits on annual construction programs, but the negotiations came to nothing. In the end, the Germans accepted the fact that the British would always have a larger navy.

THE SECOND HAGUE PEACE CONFERENCE CONVENES

> *Though the 1907 gathering at The Hague was called the "Second International Peace Conference," the main topics of discussion and negotiation turned out to be the rules of warfare.*

Threats to World Peace

Since the adjournment of the International Peace Conference, or the First Hague Conference, on July 29, 1899, there had been no indication that the world's Great Powers—including France, Germany, Great Britain, Japan, Russia, and the United States—were willing to sacrifice what they saw as their own interests in order to create peace. Great Britain had involved itself in the Boer War, the Great Powers had joined to suppress the Boxer Rebellion in China, and sporadic fighting had occurred in the Philippines.

The country most of the other powers feared, however, was Germany. In 1900, Germany had decided to begin a massive program to build warships. This "Naval Law," if fully carried out, would have meant that within twenty years Great Britain's supremacy at sea would be in serious doubt.

In response, Great Britain began to make alliances with other nations: the Hay-Paunceforte Treaty with the United States in 1901, an alliance with Japan in 1902, and the Entente Cordiale with France in 1904. Also, Arthur James Balfour, Prime Minister of Great Britain from 1902 to 1905, had taken steps to modernize the British naval and military forces.

This series of events made the world's balance of power seem more shaky than ever. In 1905, there was a crisis in Morocco, one of the areas in North Africa where European colonial rivalries were especially intense. William II, Emperor of Germany, was blamed for the crisis. In the same year, Japan had surprised the world with its easy victories over Russia at Port Arthur and Mukden,

What: International relations
When: June, 1907
Where: The Hague, the Netherlands
Who:
THEODORE ROOSEVELT (1858-1919), President of the United States from 1901 to 1909
ELIHU ROOT (1845-1937), U.S. Secretary of State from 1905 to 1909
NICHOLAS II (1868-1918), Czar of Russia from 1894 to 1917
ALEKSANDR PETROVICH IZVOLSKI (1856-1919), Russian Minister of Foreign Affairs
SIR HENRY CAMPBELL-BANNERMAN (1836-1908), Prime Minister of Great Britain from 1905 to 1908
SIR EDWARD GREY (1862-1933), Foreign Secretary of Great Britain from 1905 to 1916
WILLIAM II (1859-1941), Emperor of Germany from 1888 to 1918
JOSEPH HODGES CHOATE (1832-1917), chief delegate from the United States to the Second Hague Peace Conference

humiliating Russia even further in defeating the Russian Baltic Fleet in the Tsushima Strait.

Talk of Peace and War

World leaders who favored peace and disarmament began to ask for a second International

Peace Conference at The Hague to deal with many questions that had not been resolved in the 1899 conference. Having helped to negotiate a settlement to the Russo-Japanese War, U.S. President Theodore Roosevelt seemed the obvious sponsor. Yet Nicholas II, Czar of Russia, who wanted to regain influence and prestige after the embarrassment of losing to the Japanese, was the one who issued the invitations.

Russia and Germany made it known from the beginning that they had no intention of discussing disarmament or the limiting of arms. William II said that if disarmament were brought up at all in the conference, his delegates would leave, while Aleksandr Petrovich Izvolski, Russian Minister of Foreign Affairs, called disarmament "a craze of Jews, Socialists and hysterical women."

Though Elihu Root, U.S. Secretary of State, thought that disarmament and related questions should be discussed, Roosevelt considered it fairly worthless to do so. The United States was pursuing the building of battleships of the *Dreadnought* class, and Roosevelt claimed that they would be a greater deterrent to war than any peace society.

It cannot be surprising, then, that the Second Hague Conference focused more on ways of conducting war than on ways of creating peace. The conference opened on June 15, 1907. Forty-four nations were represented — eighteen more than had been at the 1899 conference. The principal topics discussed were arbitration in international disputes, rules of land warfare, rules of war at sea, and maritime law. Great Britain did bring to the floor a proposal for considering disarmament or a moratorium on arms buildup, but within less than half an hour it had been voted away with the recommendation that it be given "serious study."

In wars at sea, the British strategy had been to form blockades. This practice was challenged at the conference, as was the submarine warfare that Germany had been preparing for. Yet Great Britain remained determined to keep its right to blockade harbors and capture ships, while the Germans were equally determined to use contact mines and submarines to break blockades.

In regard to the settlement of international disputes, delegates debated whether arbitration should be voluntary or required. The Germans insisted that it could not be compulsory, and in the final document — the Convention of Pacific Settlement of International Disputes — their view prevailed.

Though some of the European nations objected, the Americans pushed through a resolution specifying that the Hague conferences should continue. A third conference was to be held in another eight years, the same length of time that separated the first two conferences. By 1915, though, World War I was in full swing.

Consequences

In the first decade of the twentieth century, Great Britain, Germany, Russia, France, Japan, and the United States were all competing to prove themselves as world powers. In the race for power, the main methods were forming alliances and building up military forces and weapons.

In this international mood, a peace conference had little chance of making headway toward an actual reduction in arms. The participants in the Second Hague Conference did come to some agreements about what would and would not be permitted in conducting wars, but once World War I broke out, many of these agreements were disregarded in the heat of battle.

Though the terrible devastation of the two world wars caused many people to reconsider disarmament as a worthwhile goal, debates continue about how peace is to be kept. It has long been debated whether the best deterrent to war is a large military buildup, including the development of nuclear weapons — "peace through strength" — or a reduction of arms and a placement of greater concern on meeting important human needs.

Working for peace: President Theodore Roosevelt (center) with envoys of the mikado and the czar. (*Library of Congress*)

BRITAIN, FRANCE, AND RUSSIA FORM THE TRIPLE ENTENTE

The growing cooperation among Great Britain, Russia, and France, strengthened by the Anglo-Russian Entente signed in 1907, would prove very important with the outbreak of World War I seven years later.

What: International relations
When: August 31, 1907
Where: London and Saint Petersburg
Who:
EDWARD VII (1841-1910), King of Great Britain from 1901 to 1910
ALEKSANDR PETROVICH IZVOLSKI (1856-1919), Russian Minister of Foreign Affairs from 1906 to 1910
SIR EDWARD GREY (1862-1933), Foreign Secretary of Great Britain from 1905 to 1916
SIR CHARLES HARDINGE (1858-1944), British ambassador to Russia from 1904 to 1906 and Permanent Undersecretary at the British Foreign Office from 1906 to 1910
SIR ARTHUR NICOLSON (1849-1928), British ambassador to Russia from 1906 to 1910

The Need for Accord

During 1904 and 1905, Great Britain entered into the Entente Cordiale with France, which was already allied with Russia. At the same time, relations between Germany and Great Britain were continuing to deteriorate. The first Moroccan crisis and Germany's determination to build up its navy added to British misgivings.

Great Britain first attempted to form an alliance with Russia in April, 1904, when talks were held between King Edward VII and Aleksandr Pe-

trovich Izvolski, who at that time was Russia's envoy to Denmark.

Meanwhile, the British and French governments were completing the Entente Cordiale. Since February of that year, Russia had been at war with Japan. Japan had been an ally of Great Britain since 1902, but their agreement required one to come to the aid of the other only if that other was involved in war with two countries. Because of this requirement, Great Britain remained free to stay out of the Russo-Japanese War and to build its own alliance with Russia.

Both British Foreign Secretary Sir Edward Grey and Sir Charles Hardinge, British ambassador to Russia from 1904 to 1906, earnestly wished to settle Great Britain's differences with Russia over Persia and India. In July, 1905, Emperor William II of Germany and Czar Nicholas II of Russia signed the Björkö Treaty, agreeing that they would come to each other's aid in case of attack by another European power. German officials had wanted to extend the two countries' promises to each other through the treaty, but that goal had been opposed by the Russian Foreign Office and by leaders in France, Russia's main ally.

Concerned about the move toward friendship between Germany and Russia, Grey and Hardinge continued to press for an Anglo-Russian agreement. In 1907, they received the help of Sir Arthur Nicolson, who became the new British ambassador to Russia after Hardinge became Permanent Undersecretary at the British Foreign Office. Nicolson worked hard to write an agree-

Sir Edward Grey

Baron Hardinge

ment that the Russians could accept.

Since May, 1906, Aleksandr Izvolski had been Minister of Foreign Affairs in Russia. He had already been advocating closer ties between Russia and Great Britain, for four reasons. First, he thought such ties would allow Russia to mend its relations with Japan, which in 1905 had renewed its alliance with Great Britain. Second, he thought that an Anglo-Russian entente would strengthen Russia's alliance with France. Third, the Russians had already joined the British in expressing a desire to resolve their differences regarding Persia, India, and other parts of Asia.

Finally, if Russia and Great Britain could create ties, there would be no need for an alliance with Germany. With British and French protection, Russia could challenge German and Austrian efforts to extend influence in the Middle East, and Russian ships could eventually gain access to the Dardanelles, a strait opening to the Aegean Sea.

The Agreement Is Made

Negotiations began in June, 1906, but dragged on until August, 1907. It took time to break down the suspicions between the two countries. Nicholas II, an autocratic czar, had little in common with British Liberalism, and the British Liberal press raised an outcry against attacks on Jews in Russia and criticized the closing of the Duma, the Russian parliament.

Izvolski insisted that the Dardanelles should be open to Russian warships; he got Grey to promise only that in the future would Great Britain not oppose Russia in this regard. Izvolski accepted the British negotiators' demand that Persia be divided into British and Russian spheres of influence, though Russia had earlier wished to dominate all of Persia in order to have access to the Persian Gulf. The British government also insisted that Russia simultaneously make reconciliation with Japan; on July 30, 1907, Russia and Japan signed a treaty agreeing to respect each other's rights in the Far East. A month later, Izvolski and Nicolson signed the convention that established the Anglo-Russian Entente.

The entente had to do only with Asia—specifically Afghanistan, Tibet, and Persia. With the Russian promise that each should respect the territorial integrity of Tibet (which was ruled by China) and of Afghanistan, Great Britain was assured that these two states would stand in the way of any future Russian advance toward India, one of Great Britain's important colonies.

Even more important was the agreement to recognize the "independence" and "integrity" of Persia while dividing it up into three spheres of influence. Russia received the northern zone, which was the largest but did not include the Persian Gulf. The gulf was declared to be a neutral zone. The British received a desert wasteland in the south that contained roads leading to India.

The agreement contained no commitment of the two nations to fight for each other in case of war. Still, the Anglo-Russian agreement completed a network of treaties that bound together Great Britain, Russia, and France. Newspapers in these countries began to call this network the "Triple Entente."

Consequences

The agreement did not create immediate cooperation and understanding on many issues. Great Britain's commitments to France and Russia were limited, and the agreement had to do only with Asia. Yet it did do away with some of the conflict between the British and the Russians.

The Anglo-Russian Entente was important as a step toward cooperation among Great Britain, France, and Russia—a cooperation that became more important in the next few years. Crises in Morocco and the Balkans drew these three powers together in opposition to Germany and Austria-Hungary. The members of the Triple Entente began to do some of their military planning together, anticipating a serious conflict with Germany. Those preparations served them well when they entered World War I as allies in 1914.

MULLER V. OREGON UPHOLDS SOCIOLOGICAL JURISPRUDENCE

> *In this important case, the Supreme Court agreed that the constitutionality of laws should be judged not only by legal precedent but also by their effect on people's well-being.*

Defeat of Reform Laws

At the beginning of the twentieth century, many — perhaps most — lawyers and judges in the United States believed in "natural" economic laws and held that property rights were more important than human rights. According to their thinking, judges in the United States were entitled to review legislation to see whether it agreed with or violated state or federal constitutions. To attempt to control the use of property through laws, these people said, *was* unconstitutional and went against the natural order of things.

Labor leaders and social reformers working to improve the welfare of poor working people had begun to see the courts, then, as the greatest threat to progress. When states had passed laws attempting to improve people's living and working conditions, federal courts had often struck them down. In addition, the Supreme Court had accepted the idea that corporations were persons under the Fourteenth Amendment. No state, it said, could deprive a corporation (person) of life, liberty, or property without due process of law.

In 1905, the Supreme Court set specific limitations on how far a state could go in making laws about hours and other working conditions for its industrial laborers. In *Lochner* v. *New York*, the Supreme Court ruled that laws such as a New York law to limit the working hours of bakers to ten hours per day and sixty hours per week were "mere meddlesome interferences with the rights of the individual." A state could not interfere with the freedom of employer and employee to make a labor contract unless there were obvious important reasons such as health.

What: Law and labor
When: 1908
Where: Washington, D.C.
Who:
Louis Dembitz Brandeis (1856-1941), an American lawyer
Florence Kelley (1859-1932), General Secretary of the National Consumers' League, and a social reformer
Josephine Goldmark (1877-1950), a leader of the National Consumers' League

Social reformers became alarmed that state restrictions on the working hours of women might also be in danger. Thus it was that Florence Kelley, Chief Factory Inspector of Illinois and General Secretary of the National Consumers' League, joined Josephine Goldmark, another leader in the National Consumers' League, to hire Louis Dembitz Brandeis to defend an Oregon law that limited a workday to ten hours for women workers in industry.

The Arguments

Brandeis, known as "the people's attorney," had tried for years to show that American law in his day did not match the new economic and social facts of life in America. Lawyers and judges who cared only for legal precedents and natural law knew very little about industrial conditions in the twentieth century. Brandeis said, "A lawyer who has not studied economics and soci-

ology is very apt to become a public enemy." He held that the law was a living organism that could be changed and adjusted to fit people's real lives in American cities and factories. In his brief in *Muller* v. *Oregon*, Brandeis saw an opportunity to prove the validity of what has been called "sociological jurisprudence" — taking economic and social considerations into account, as well as legal precedents, in deciding the constitutionality of a law.

Brandeis' arguments from legal precedent took up only two pages of his brief (the document that laid out his argument). In more than one hundred pages, he attempted to show that Oregon had adopted its ten-hour law for women in order to guard the public health, safety, and welfare. "Long hours of labor are dangerous for women," Brandeis said, more than for men, because of physiological differences. "Overwork . . . is more dangerous to the health of women than of men, and entails upon them more lasting injury." When working women became very fatigued, he went on, there was often a "general deterioration of health" — anemia, difficulties in childbearing, and industrial accidents.

Furthermore, he said, overwork was demoralizing. A breakdown in the health and morals of women "inevitably lowers the entire community physically, mentally, and morally." There would be a rise in infant mortality, he predicted, if women were forced to work long hours. On the other hand, he argued that reasonable working hours actually raised "the tone of the entire community."

Brandeis brought together his economic and social evidence in a very convincing presentation. In response, the Court decided to uphold Oregon's ten-hour law for women.

Consequences

Several years later, attorney and law professor Felix Frankfurter wrote, "The *Muller* case is epoch-making, not because of its decision, but because of the authoritative recognition by the Supreme Court that the way in which Mr. Brandeis presented the case . . . laid down a new technique for counsel." When constitutional questions were being argued, Frankfurter said, courts were now obligated to insist on considering social and economic effects before deciding the issue.

Brandeis himself continued to learn about the realities of life among the American working class, and he became an expert in labor economics. In 1916, President Woodrow Wilson nominated him to serve on the Supreme Court. Though the appointment was bitterly fought by conservatives, Brandeis eventually took his seat on the Court, where he was able to help shape the direction of American law for twenty-three years. His principles of sociological jurisprudence have been a basic part of legal and constitutional practice ever since.

Austria Annexes Bosnia and Hercegovina

> When Austria-Hungary annexed two Serbo-Croatian countries that it had administered since 1878 under the terms of the Congress of Berlin, other European powers reacted with anger but, in the end, allowed the annexation to stand.

What: International relations
When: October 7, 1908
Where: The Balkans
Who:
Count Alois Lexa von Aehrenthal (1854-1912), Foreign Minister of Austria-Hungary from 1906 to 1912
Aleksandr Petrovich Izvolski (1856-1919), Russian Minister of Foreign Affairs from 1906 to 1910
Pëtr Arkadevich Stolypin (1862-1911), Premier of Russia from 1906 to 1911
Sir Edward Grey (1862-1933), Foreign Secretary of Great Britain from 1905 to 1916
Prince Bernhard von Bülow (1849-1929), Chancellor of the German Empire from 1900 to 1909

Secret Negotiations

Bosnia and Hercegovina, Balkan states which were predominantly Serbo-Croatian, had been under the rule of Austria since 1878, according to the terms of the Congress of Berlin. Serbia, a neighboring nation, had been ruled since 1903 by Peter I, of the Karageorgevich dynasty, which was traditionally hostile to Austria. With the Serbian Radical Party in power, Serbia aimed to gather all the southern Slav countries under Habsburg control into a greater Serbian or Yugoslav state. Alois Lexa von Aehrenthal, who had been appointed Foreign Minister of Austria-Hungary in 1906, was well aware of Serbia's ambitions. He believed that Austria-Hungary should annex Bosnia and Hercegovina so as to frustrate Serbian efforts to dominate the region.

With the knowledge of Czar Nicholas II but not the government, the Russian Minister of Foreign Affairs, Aleksandr Petrovich Izvolski, secretly let Aehrenthal know that Russia would be willing to support Austria-Hungary's annexation of Bosnia and Hercegovina. There was, however, one condition: Austria-Hungary, also known as the Dual Monarchy, must approve the opening of the Dardanelles Strait to Russian warships. Aehrenthal received this proposal positively, and the two statesmen then awaited the right moment to seal their bargain.

That moment came in the summer of 1908, with the outbreak of the Young Turk Revolution. The goal of this uprising was to revive the Ottoman Empire, especially in the Balkans. While the Turks were preoccupied with civil war, Aehrenthal and Izvolski met in Buchlau, Moravia, on September 15 and orally repeated their earlier agreement to support each other's aims in the Balkans. Unfortunately, they made no written account of their decisions, nor did they set a date for the annexation. As a result, within three weeks a serious misunderstanding led to a crisis in Europe.

The Annexation

Izvolski left the conference with the impression that nothing would be done immediately (or so he

The marketplace of Sarajevo, Bosnia, Austria-Hungary, c. 1910. (*Library of Congress*)

later claimed). He set out to visit various European capitals to try to obtain the Great Powers' agreement to Russia's upcoming access to the Dardanelles.

Meanwhile, Aehrenthal was preparing for the annexation. He told Bulgaria that it should proclaim its independence, which it did on October 5. Two days later, Aehrenthal announced that Austria had annexed Bosnia and Hercegovina.

The protest that arose was so great that it brought Austria to the brink of war with the other European nations. Serbia and Montenegro were outraged, viewing the annexation as a deliberate step to make sure that a great southern Slav state would not be formed. The Young Turks were angry at Austria's violation of Ottoman sovereignty.

In Russia, where there was much sympathy with the southern Slavs, the annexation and Izvolski's role in helping to make it possible were loudly condemned. Pëtr Arkadevich Stolypin, Premier of Russia, ordered Izvolski to retract his support for the annexation. Izvolski did so by denying any involvement and by calling on Great Britain and France to come to the aid of Serbia and the Turks.

That help, however, did not come. France and Great Britain were not pleased with the annexation, but they recognized the fact that Austria-Hungary had been in control of Bosnia and Hercegovina for thirty years already, so the status quo in the western Balkans would not really be changed much. Sir Edward Grey, the British Foreign Secretary, did reject Izvolski's plea for

the opening of the Dardanelles to Russian warships.

Relations among the European states remained in a crisis for almost six months. With the reluctant support of Russia, Serbia prepared for war with Austria. Izvolski insisted that the dispute be brought before an international conference, while Aehrenthal firmly refused.

Great Britain and France did not give strong support to Russia, but Germany's decision to give full support to its ally Austria-Hungary finally brought the crisis to an end. On March 21, 1909, Prince Bernhard von Bülow, Chancellor of the German Empire, practically ordered Izvolski to back down and accept the annexation. Izvolski did so, and on March 31, 1909, Serbia very reluctantly followed suit.

Consequences

Though peace was restored to the Balkans, it was a shaky peace that lasted for only a few years. Relations between Austria and Serbia got progressively worse, until Archduke Francis Ferdinand of Austria was assassinated in 1914, by a Serbian nationalist.

Meanwhile, the uneasy truce that Austria and Russia had maintained in the Balkans from 1878 to 1908, was now shattered beyond repair. After 1908, Russian diplomats worked hard to create a league of Balkan states as a barrier against any Austrian ambitions to expand the Austro-Hungarian empire further. A Balkan League was indeed founded in 1912; yet instead of uniting against Austria, it used its strength to disrupt the Ottoman Empire still further.

THE BELGIAN GOVERNMENT ANNEXES THE CONGO

Because Africans had been mistreated under the reign of King Leopold II, the Belgian government took control of the Congo and reformed it.

Colonial Abuses

The Congo Independent State (also called the Congo Free State) was different from any other European colony in Africa. It was considered a sovereign country and was ruled by King Leopold II of Belgium, but the constitution made no link between Belgium and the Congo State until 1908. Mostly, the Congo was run as Leopold's private business.

From the time he gained control of the Congo in the 1870's, Leopold announced that he wanted to end the slave trade and bring commerce, prosperity, and "civilization" to the Africans. The Congo State did work to stop the slave trade, but otherwise Leopold did not show much concern for the rights of Africans.

The Congo Independent State ruled by military force. All land considered "unoccupied" was taken over by the government. Local officials were allowed to collect taxes as they wished, and many of them required payments of ivory, groundnuts, and wild rubber. Other taxes had to be paid in labor: cutting wood for river steamers, transporting officials in canoes, or serving as porters on expeditions. Women had to provide cassava bread for the state's workers and soldiers, and residents also had to bring meat and fish to the government stations. Naturally, villages that were close to government stations carried the heaviest tax burden.

Those who had invested money in the Congo, including Leopold, tried to get quick profits. Beginning in the early 1890's, Leopold allowed private firms to take control of vast territories. The state held half of the stock in many of these

What: Human rights and political reform
When: November 1, 1908
Where: Brussels, Belgium, and the Congo (Zaire)
Who:
LEOPOLD II (1835-1909), King of Belgium from 1865 to 1909, and founder of the Congo Independent State
EDMOND DENE MOREL (1873-1924), a British journalist
JULES RENKIN (1862-1934), Belgian Minister for Colonies from 1908 to 1918

companies, which included the Société Anversoise du Commerce du Congo (known as Anversoise), the Anglo-Belgian India Rubber and Exploring Company (called Abir), and the Compagnie du Kasai.

The worst abuses of Africans occurred in the rubber industry. Local officials set quotas of wild rubber that each village was required to produce; these officials were given a commission on the amount gathered. Soon missionaries began reporting that to punish the villagers for not meeting their quotas, the officials and their assistants were taking hostages (especially women), whipping people, and sometimes amputating their hands.

Protest Rises

In the outside world, these reports led to an outcry against the Congo State. Leopold tried to

prevent the publication of a report by British consul Roger Casement, but it was published in 1904. In response, British journalist Edmond Dene Morel founded the Congo Reform Association (CRA). Morel's campaign soon spread to other countries, especially the United States.

Finally, Leopold formed a commission to look into Casement's accusations. This commission decided that there was no evidence that European officials had ordered mutilation or murder; they claimed that the amputations were the result of a "native custom." Nevertheless, the commission's report, released in 1905, did back up most of Casement's findings.

According to the commission, there were abuses in the tax system, the companies in the Congo were not well supervised, and unauthorized military expeditions were being sent out by the companies. Leopold set up another commission to recommend reforms.

Meanwhile, the push for reform was gaining steam overseas. Sir Edward Grey, who had already criticized the Congo State, became Foreign Secretary of Great Britain. By 1906, the Hearst newspapers in the United States had taken up the campaign against Leopold. A reform movement also appeared in Belgium itself, as the Socialist Party gained strength in the parliament.

By 1906, Belgium was being pressured hard by other nations. Leopold introduced reforms in that year, but Morel and the CRA said that they were not enough. In November, Grey told a group of reformers that he hoped Belgium would annex the Congo. In December, the Belgian parliament debated the issue and voted to consider annexation.

Negotiations with Leopold were long and difficult, but a treaty was finally written to transfer the Congo to Belgium, along with a new colonial charter. The Belgian Chambers made these documents into law in August and September, 1908. The annexation came into effect on November 1, 1908, although it was not announced in the Congo until November 16.

Consequences

Morel was not satisfied with the annexation, for King Leopold still had certain powers in the new Belgian Congo. The companies that had invested in the Congo were allowed to remain, although their powers of administration were reduced. The new colonial law did not bring an end to forced labor, and most of Leopold's officials continued in their jobs. So Morel and the CRA convinced the British and American governments not to recognize the annexation immediately.

Because of the efforts of Morel and of Jules Renkin, the new Belgian minister of colonies, there were soon reforms in the Belgian Congo. Renkin presented his reform program in October, 1909. Free trade would be introduced over a period of three years, and consumer goods would be imported for Africans. Taxes would now be paid in currency.

In December, 1909, Leopold died. His successor, Albert I, wanted to encourage humane policies in Africa and had even visited the colony himself — something Leopold had never done. In 1912, Renkin was given the power to remove officials who were corrupt; that same year, the old governor, Baron Théophile Wahis, was replaced. In June, 1913, the CRA dissolved itself, having decided that its job was done. The United States and Great Britain granted recognition to the Belgian Congo.

Gradually, the Belgian Congo became similar to other European colonies in Africa. The Europeans discriminated against the Africans, who still had few rights under the law and no voice in government. For the most part, they were not subjected to open cruelty. The government gave subsidies to mission schools for Africans, but discouraged them from getting a more advanced education.

Under this "paternalistic" system, adult Africans were treated as children. When independence came suddenly to the Belgian Congo in 1960, the frustrations of years of European rule were expressed in a long, bloody civil war.

Leopold II, King of Belgium. (*Library of Congress*)

57

THE NATIONAL ASSOCIATION FOR THE ADVANCEMENT OF COLORED PEOPLE IS FORMED

The NAACP was founded as a national organization that would promote the rights of African Americans.

What: Social and political reform
When: 1909
Where: New York City
Who:
WILLIAM EDWARD BURGHARDT DU BOIS (1868-1963), a professor at Atlanta University
BOOKER TALIAFERRO WASHINGTON (1856-1915), the founder and president of Tuskegee Institute
WILLIAM MONROE TROTTER (1872-1934), a radical African-American leader
WILLIAM ENGLISH WALLING (1877-1936), a journalist and labor organizer

Rights Under Attack

By the beginning of the twentieth century, many of the civil rights achieved by African Americans during the Reconstruction period were under severe attack. Supported by Supreme Court rulings in their favor, Southern states passed laws that had the effect of taking away the vote from most African-American citizens. Other laws promoted segregation—preventing African Americans from using and participating in public institutions on an equal basis with whites.

In the North, white people were generally not as open in practicing racial discrimination, but it was still taken for granted. Tensions between the two races sometimes erupted into violence—

lynchings or riots in the cities. In these confrontations, African Americans received little help from the press, the courts, and the law-enforcement agencies.

Within the African-American community, there were various opinions about how to respond to the loss of rights. The most prominent spokesman for African Americans, educator Booker T. Washington, had for some time been urging people of color to work on getting skills and education so they could gain better jobs in factories and businesses. For the time being, he said, these goals should take priority over the push for civil and political rights.

Professor W. E. B. Du Bois, at Atlanta University, disagreed with Washington. In 1905, Du Bois founded the Niagara Movement, an organization of well-educated African Americans who called for public protest against the loss of rights. They did not think it was right to ignore discrimination and merely try to get good jobs. Du Bois' point of view was the one that inspired a group of people in 1909 to start an organization dedicated to fighting racial discrimination in all areas of American life.

The NAACP Is Born

In August, 1908, there was a bloody race riot in Springfield, Illinois. White mobs destroyed much of the black section of Springfield and lynched two African Americans. More than fifty others were left dead or injured, and about two thousand African-American residents left the city.

Shocked that the hometown of Abraham Lincoln could be the site of such violence, a group of

58

W. E. B. Du Bois. (*Library of Congress*)

white liberals decided that something should be done. William English Walling, a Kentucky journalist and labor organizer, wrote several articles in *The Independent*, condemning the Springfield riot and calling for "a powerful body of citizens" to come to the aid of African Americans.

Early in 1909, Walling met with Mary White Ovington, the Socialist descendant of an Abolitionist family, and Henry Moskovitz, a New York social worker, to discuss ways of gaining support for his idea. They invited Oswald Garrison Villard (grandson of William Lloyd Garrison, a famous Abolitionist) to join them, and the group soon grew to more than fifteen, including two prominent African-American clergymen, Bishop Alexander Walters and the Reverend William Henry Brooks.

This planning committee decided to hold a "Conference on the Status of the Negro" on May 31 and June 1 in New York City. About three hundred men and women, including many white liberals, attended the two-day meeting. There they established a permanent organization and listened to scientific evidence to disprove the idea that black people were genetically inferior to whites. Du Bois presented a speech in which he argued that the problems of African Americans were as much political as economic—that is, it was not simply that African Americans were poor but also that they were being treated unfairly under the current laws and government.

Booker T. Washington had been invited to the conference but had been told that the new organization would be an aggressive one. He decided not to attend. Yet his absence did not mean that there was complete agreement on what was to be done. There were heated arguments before the selection of a Committee of Forty on Permanent Organization, and before resolutions were passed demanding equal rights for African Americans and protection against violence. Villard's proposals were opposed strongly by William Monroe Trotter, editor of the *Boston Guardian*, and by J. Milton Waldron, president of the National Negro

Political League. Both of these leaders favored more radical positions than those adopted by the majority, and in the end, neither of them was chosen for the Committee of Forty.

During the next year, Villard and others struggled to raise funds and plan for a second conference. Though the white press generally ignored them, and though there were open disputes with Washington, the committee succeeded in making a plan for organizing the new group so that it could move forward in its task.

At the second annual conference, the group, now named the National Association for the Advancement of Colored People, appointed Du Bois as director of publicity and research. In making this choice the organization clearly identified itself as progressive. Du Bois had been frustrated with his own Niagara Movement and saw his new post as a chance to become more effective as a spokesman for change. Within six months, he had launched the NAACP magazine, *Crisis*, which soon became an important opinion maker on issues of race.

Consequences

For the first time since Reconstruction, there was a major drive to end discrimination against African Americans in the United States. The way the NAACP was formed reflected many of the strengths and weaknesses that continued to mark the organization in its first few years. There were a large number of white leaders, and the organization depended on financial support from white liberals. Its program emphasized political and civil rights and aimed for change by means of laws and court decisions.

There were those within the African-American community who criticized the NAACP for these characteristics. In the early years, most of the protests came from those who believed that the new organization was too aggressive. Even at the beginning, however, there were also some, such as Trotter, who insisted that the NAACP did not go far enough in pressing for change.

TAFT CONDUCTS DOLLAR DIPLOMACY

In a cooperative effort between American government and business, President William Howard Taft began a policy of using business investments to try to bring stability to struggling nations.

Dollars Instead of Bullets

The policy that has become known as "dollar diplomacy" was begun by President William Howard Taft and his Secretary of State, Philander C. Knox. A lawyer from Pennsylvania, Knox was sympathetic to big business but was also concerned to build support for the United States within other nations and their governments. The best way to help both American business and American government, Taft and Knox decided, was to bring American money and business know-how to countries whose support for the United States was important and that needed help to improve their economy and standard of living.

This kind of American intervention would be peaceful — sending dollars instead of bullets — and American companies and foreign populations would both benefit. In 1910, Knox said, "The problem of good government is inextricably interwoven with that of economic prosperity and sound finance; financial stability contributes perhaps more than any other one factor to political stability." If Americans brought money and jobs to other countries, Knox believed, the governments of those countries would become more stable and would be better allies of the United States.

Testing the Theory

The Taft Administration used dollar diplomacy in two areas, the Caribbean and China. In the Caribbean, Taft and Knox followed the program begun by Theodore Roosevelt's administration in the Dominican Republic. That country had been politically unstable, and American officials had

What: Economics and international relations
When: 1909-1913
Where: Washington, D.C.
Who:
WILLIAM HOWARD TAFT (1857-1930), President of the United States from 1909 to 1913
PHILANDER CHASE KNOX (1835-1921), U.S. Secretary of State from 1909 to 1913

feared that foreign nations would take advantage of the situation and try to take control there. So it was that in 1905, Roosevelt had made an agreement with leaders of the Dominican Republic. The Dominican government would receive a loan from American banks to pay off its debts. In exchange for the loan, the American president would be allowed to appoint the head of the Dominican customs service — and in the Dominican Republic, as in all Caribbean states, the customs service was the main source of income for the government. The arrangement seemed to work perfectly. After the Americans took over the collection of customs money, the Dominican Republic enjoyed a time of peace, and the financial situation of its government improved. This state of affairs lasted through most of the Taft presidency.

Taft and Knox tried to use the same principles in dealing with Nicaragua. After supporting the overthrow of the powerful dictator José Santos Zelaya in 1909, Taft sent Thomas C. Dawson to

Nicaragua to help the new government restore order. Dawson persuaded the Nicaraguans to install an American collector of customs and, in return, obtained a loan for Nicaragua from New York banks. Though the U.S. Senate refused several times to ratify this agreement, Taft appointed a collector of customs by executive order, and the New York bankers made several loans to Nicaragua. As extra security for the loans, the American banks took a controlling interest in the Nicaraguan National Bank and the Nicaraguan state railways.

In spite of these efforts to make Nicaragua financially stable, in 1912 the country's majority political party began a revolt against the American-supported President Adolfo Díaz. The Taft Administration responded by sending warships and marines to keep Díaz in power. Unfortunately, bullets along with dollars were needed to keep Nicaragua in the kind of order that the U.S. government wanted to see.

The situation in China was quite different from that of the Caribbean. In China there was more active competition for political and economic influence, and the United States had less influence there than did several other Great Powers. Under Roosevelt, the American policy in the Far East had depended upon good relations with Japan: Japanese cooperation was considered essential to protect the Philippines as an American possession. In dealing with China, then, dollar diplomacy represented a major change in U.S. policy.

Taft and Knox tried to increase American influence in China mainly by funneling American money into that country. Their approach never changed. They demanded that American banking groups be included equally with banks from other countries in backing every foreign loan floated by China. Yet the New York bankers Taft had relied upon in Nicaragua did not have as much interest in investing in China, and they also did not have enough money at their disposal to make the large investments the Taft Administration was seeking. To raise the money, the American banks had to

rely on loans from the money markets of Great Britain and France. Thus the "American" investment in China was not really American.

Because American funds for investing in China were hard to come by, and because other world powers were unhappy with U.S. attempts to compete there, in 1912 the Taft Administration decided not to continue its aggressive financial involvement in China. Instead, the United States returned to the more moderate "open door" approach of earlier administrations.

Consequences

The attempt to use dollar diplomacy in Nicaragua showed that Taft and Knox's thinking was too simplistic. Political stability there did not depend only on paying debts and keeping up with budgets. Other important factors in Nicaraguan political life were political rivalry, struggles for prestige and power, the large gap in standard of living between a wealthy few and many poor, and resentment against American interference. All these factors worked against Taft's efforts from the very beginning.

Even the Dominican Republic, considered the "model" of dollar diplomacy, actually had succeeded not because of American policy but because of a skillful president, Roman Caceras. When Caceras was assassinated, a new wave of unrest arose in the Dominican Republic, and it was ended only in 1916, when the United States Marines occupied the capital city and other important areas of the country.

Dollar diplomacy, then, was not nearly as successful as some have made it out to be. It did bring the United States forward as one of the world's imperialistic powers in the years before World War I. Dollar diplomacy was part of the long history of U.S. interventions south of its borders—interventions that created great tensions between the United States and Latin American countries in the second half of the twentieth century.

William Howard Taft. (*White House Historical Association*)

63

THE MEXICAN REVOLUTION ENDS IN CONSTITUTIONAL GOVERNMENT

> *The Mexican Revolution succeeded in gaining broader representation in government for the people.*

What: Civil war, military conflict, and political reform
When: The 1910's
Where: Mexico
Who:
PORFIRIO DÍAZ (1830-1915), President of Mexico from 1876 to 1880 and 1884 to 1911
FRANCISCO INDALECIO MADERO (1873-1913), a leader in the Mexican Revolution, and President of Mexico from 1911 to 1913
VICTORIANO DE LA HUERTA (1854-1916), Provisional President of Mexico from 1913 to 1914
VENUSTIANO CARRANZA (1859-1920), a leader of the Constitutionalist Movement, and President of Mexico from 1914 to 1920
ÁLVARO OBREGÓN (1880-1928), a major figure in the Constitutionalist Movement, and President of Mexico from 1920 to 1924
FRANCISCO (PANCHO) VILLA (1877-1923) and
EMILIANO ZAPATA (1877?-1919), popular revolutionary leaders

The Díaz Regime

In 1876 Mexico had come under the rule of Porfirio Díaz, whose motto had been the restoration of constitutional government. Although he did operate under a constitution, he dominated the country as a dictator. He allowed large groups of Mexicans to lose important political and economic rights.

Díaz invited investors from foreign countries to bring their wealth to Mexico. Wealthy U.S. investors were happy to accept the invitation at a time when railroads, mining (especially of petroleum), and land were all being developed in Mexico. Petroleum production increased more than a thousandfold between 1901 and 1911, under mostly American control. This industry was almost completely free from taxes during Díaz' regime. Foreign individuals and companies also invested in land, sometimes establishing large haciendas (ranches) that spread across millions of acres.

Reform and Revolution

More and more, Díaz was criticized within Mexico for dominating the country and failing to protect the people's political rights. A challenge to his presidency came in the election of 1910, when Francisco Madero ran against Díaz. When Madero lost, he called the election fraudulent and declared himself in revolt. His protest encouraged others to rise up against Díaz. In 1911, the regime fell from power, and Díaz went into exile; Madero was elected the new president.

Yet Madero kept many of the Díaz officials in power, and his middle-of-the-road policies did not satisfy either the *porfiristas* (those loyal to Díaz) or those who wanted sweeping change in Mexico. There were various rebellions, and finally, Gen-

General Venustiano Carranza (with beard) in the field with his staff. (*Library of Congress*)

eral Victoriano Huerta led a successful overthrow of Madero in February, 1913. Madero and his vice president were killed.

Huerta, a *porfirista*, came under immediate attack from liberals and revolutionaries across Mexico. In the south there was an uprising led by Emiliano Zapata, while in the north another band of revolutionaries gathered around Pancho Villa. At one time, more than two hundred "revolutionary" groups claimed to be the legitimate government of Mexico.

Zapata issued his Plan of Ayala, calling for reform in agriculture and the ownership of land. His supporters were mostly Indians and peasants. Villa, based in the northern state of Chihuahua, was a very independent leader, but he did fight alongside the Constitutionalists (or *carrancistas*), led by Venustiano Carranza. Carranza issued the Plan of Guadalupe, which called for the restoration of constitutional government in Mexico.

These men's groups, along with many others, succeeded in overthrowing Huerta in August, 1914. Within a short time, however, the leaders of the various revolutionary factions were fighting among themselves.

Carranza and the Constitutionalists won in the end for two reasons. One was the unusual talent of Carranza's ally Álvaro Obregón, a military leader who defeated Villa in April, 1915, and became known as the Hero of Celaya. Obregón was a very persuasive man who was able to attract the Mexican labor movement and other important groups to support the Constitutionalists. The second reason for Carranza's success was that the Woodrow Wilson Administration gave recognition to his government in October, 1915.

Though Carranza never united all Mexico under his government, he did have several important successes. Most important, in the fall of 1916 he authorized the calling of a convention to write a new constitution for Mexico. This constitution made use of some of the more revolutionary ideas, such as land reform, labor reform, reform of the petroleum and other mining industries, and restrictions on the powers of the Roman Catholic clergy. Clearly, it not only offered political free-

doms but also launched major changes in Mexico's economic system and the living conditions of its people.

Carranza himself was not committed to the more radical changes promised by the constitution. Many Mexicans began to criticize him for not fulfilling promises he had made since 1913, and he was blamed for the continuing civil strife, crime, and corruption in the country. Villa and Zapata were still leading armed uprisings against his government. In 1919, however, Carranza "solved" one problem by allowing some *carrancistas* to assassinate Zapata.

The constitution did not allow presidents to have more than one term in office, so Carranza chose Ignacio Bonillas, Mexico's ambassador to the United States, to succeed him in 1920. This decision was a serious mistake. The logical candidate for the presidency was Obregón, a national hero who was spoken of as "a genius in war and peace." Obregón had announced his own candidacy in June, 1919. Trying to thwart him, Carranza ordered federal troops to move into Sonora, which was the base of Obregón's power. As a result, a new revolutionary movement appeared on the scene, led by Obregón and a few other Sonorans.

Their political program, the Plan of Agua Prieta, was proclaimed on April 23, 1920, and rebuked Carranza for trying to impose a president on Mexico by force. He was declared unfit for office, and the revolutionaries moved to seize power and appoint a provisional president. Carranza fled the capital and was killed on May 21, 1920. Adolfo de la Huerta became provisional president until November 30, 1920, and succeeded in making an agreement with Villa so that he would stop his attacks on the government.

Meanwhile, Obregón was elected president; he took office on December 1, 1920. His election marked the end of the Mexican Revolution and brought calm to the country.

Consequences

The Mexican Revolution — which began with Madero's attempt to succeed Díaz as Mexico's president — launched a reform movement that led to the social, economic, and political reorganization of the country. Though the revolutionaries did not succeed in making all the changes they had hoped to make, there was some evidence of real and lasting change. The government of Mexico had been given to the common people. Wealthy people of Spanish descent no longer held exclusive power; Mexicans of *mestizo* (mixed Indian and Spanish) background were now well represented. Land was eventually redistributed, especially under the government of Lázaro Cárdenas, who was president from 1934 to 1940.

THE UNION OF SOUTH AFRICA IS ESTABLISHED

Four European colonies in southern Africa came together to form the Union of South Africa, intended as "a self-governing white community, supported by . . . black labour."

Afrikaner versus English

In the nineteenth century, the two most serious problems within South Africa were political unity among the whites (South Africans of English and Dutch descent), and what the whites called "native policy." The end of the Boer War of 1902 (what the Boers, or Dutch settlers, called the Second War of Freedom and the Africans called the White Man's War), left Great Britain with a few problems to resolve. Though the British had won the war, Africans (blacks and people of mixed race) outnumbered whites within South Africa, and the defeated Afrikaners (Boers) outnumbered whites of English origin. Leaders of both political parties in Great Britain agreed that established white communities in the British Empire should run their own affairs. How could British supremacy be established, then, within South Africa?

Great Britain's High Commissioner for South Africa, Sir Alfred Milner, had a solution: The region should become "a self-governing white community, supported by well-treated and justly governed black labour from Cape Town to Zambesi." To make sure that white South Africans remained loyal to the British Empire, Milner proposed that large numbers of British people be encouraged to move to South Africa and share in the wealth of its natural resources (which included extensive gold fields). Meanwhile, the Afrikaners could be persuaded to loosen their ties to Dutch culture.

General Horatio Herbert Kitchener, who had been British commander in chief in the Boer War, and Joseph Chamberlain, Secretary of State for

What: Political independence and reform
When: May 31, 1910
Where: South Africa
Who:
SIR ALFRED MILNER (1954-1925), Great Britain's High Commissioner for South Africa
GENERAL HORATIO HERBERT KITCHENER (1950-1916), British commander in chief in the Boer War and negotiator for Great Britain after the war
JOSEPH CHAMBERLAIN (1836-1914), British Secretary of State for the Colonies
LOUIS BOTHA (1862-1919), Prime Minister of the Transvaal (1907-1910) and first Prime Minister of the Union of South Africa (1910-1919); cofounder of *Het Volk*
JAN CHRISTIAN SMUTS (1870-1950), State Attorney for the Cape Colony and cofounder of *Het Volk*

the Colonies, wanted to treat both the Afrikaners and the Africans more liberally. In the drafting of the 1902 Treaty of Vereeniging, Milner's views won out. Yet making his ideas a reality was not easy. There was an economic recession after the Boer War, and the great wave of British immigration did not occur. Furthermore, the terms of the treaty and the way British diplomacy was carried out encouraged the Afrikaners to be even more nationalistic — and more hostile to the British — than before. As a result, the British government changed its policy to create equality between settlers of British and Dutch origin.

Forming the Union

Two Afrikaner leaders came to the fore during and just after the Boer War: Louis Botha and Jan Smuts. Botha was a farmer, while Smuts was an intellectual lawyer. Together, however, they founded a policy of *Het Volk* (the people), which stood for Afrikaner self-government along with four levels of conciliation within South Africa. First, Afrikaners were to be reconciled to one another, and second to citizens of British descent. Third, regional disputes would be solved by joining the British colonies of Cape and Natal with the Boer colonies of Transvaal and the Orange Free State. The fourth level, external conciliation,

aimed for the formation of a South African nation within a liberalized British Empire.

By 1908, Botha and Smuts had almost convinced leaders of the South African colonies that conciliation would be politically wise and morally right. Yet for the majority of South Africa's people, *Het Volk* was a white solution to a white problem. The most liberal whites in the most liberal colony (the Cape) wanted South Africa to be run along the lines of the Cape's own system — giving voting rights without any stated racial restrictions, but under other restrictions that would ensure that the vast majority of those who qualified would be white men. Smuts responded by saying that all white parties should aim "to do justice to the Natives and to take all wise and prudent measures for their civilization and improvement. But I don't believe in politics for them."

For many in the white minority the idea of union had become a top priority by 1907, for economic reasons and for self-preservation; whites wanted to build strength among themselves in order to resist rebellions among the Zulus and other African groups. Whites who were loyal to the British Empire wanted union to help lessen conflicts among the South African colonies; a unified and peaceful South Africa, they thought, might attract large numbers of British immigrants and fulfill Milner's dream of a British electoral majority. Those who were not favorable to the Empire, on the other hand, wanted union as a way for South Africa's white communities to stand together against interference from the British.

Eight years after the Peace of Vereeniging, the Union of South Africa was formed on May 31, 1910, as an independent dominion within the British Commonwealth of Nations. The four colonies — Natal, the Orange Free State, the Transvaal, and the Cape — joined the Union of South Africa. Great Britain was left with the "native territories" of Bechuanaland, Basutoland, Swaziland, and Northern and Southern Rhodesia.

The Act of Union was geared to protecting the rights and privileges of the white minority. The question of distribution of power within the white community — not the issue of the rights of Africans — had been the most debated problem. Choosing a national language was part of this problem. The decision to treat English and Afrikaans on an equal basis convinced the Afrikaners that their language and culture could be preserved within South Africa.

Consequences

The unification and independence of South Africa came at a high price for the Africans of the region, for the Act of Union made white supremacy the rule in the government of the new nation. The political and economic price is still being paid by people of color in South Africa.

African political organizations date back to 1882, but the Act of Union gave the National Native Convention a strong push to begin more open protest. As a result, the African National Congress (ANC) was formed in 1912, led by lawyers and journalists such as J. T. Javabu, who had been trained in Great Britain and the United States. The ANC remained the chief voice of South African black nationalism until it was banned in 1960 after the massacre of blacks at Sharpeville. It operated underground until 1990, when its leaders and the government of F. W. de Klerk began negotiations aimed at major political reforms within South Africa.

South Africa's Kimberley Diamond Mine c. 1905, two thousand feet underground. (*Library of Congress*) **69**

PORTUGAL BECOMES A REPUBLIC

> *With Portugal in an economic crisis as it lost its colonial holdings, Portuguese radicals overthrew the monarchy and called an assembly to draft a republican constitution.*

What: Political reform
When: October 5, 1910
Where: Lisbon, Portugal
Who:
CARLOS I (1863-1908), King of Portugal from 1889 to 1908
MANUEL II (1889-1910), King of Portugal from 1908 to 1910
TEÓFILO BRAGA (1843-1924), Provisional President of the Republic of Portugal from 1910 to 1911
AFONSO COSTA (1871-1937), Minister of Justice in 1910, who became leader of the radical Democratic Party
MANUEL JOSÉ DE ARRIAGA (1842-1917), first constitutional President of the Republic of Portugal, from 1911 to 1915
SIDÔNIO BERNARDINO CARDOSA DA SILVA PAES (1872-1918), a republican who led a coup in 1917, and became President of Portugal from 1917 to 1918
ANTONIO MACHADO DOS SANTOS (dates unknown), leader of the Carbonaria, a secret society of radical republicans

Bringing Down the Monarchy

Since the late nineteenth century, the Portuguese government had had many problems. Most of the problems had to do with money. Since Portugal had lost control of Brazil it had been unable to balance its national budget, and civil war had been very costly. There had been attempts to develop Portugal's colonies in Africa so that they would be a source of income, but British achievements in South Africa had blocked those efforts.

Much social reform was needed within Portugal. The government was full of corruption, and the results of all elections were decided in advance at the capital, Lisbon. Small socialist and republican movements raised protests against this corruption, but most of the protest was aimed at the Roman Catholic clergy, which held quite a bit of power throughout the country. The republican movement, founded by Teófilo Braga, was especially marked by fiery opposition to the clergy.

Carlos I, who had become King of Portugal in 1889, could not cope with these problems, and his ministers could not solve them. By 1905, the clamor for reform led many people to believe that the monarchy would soon be overthrown, and in 1908, Carlos and his heir were assassinated. His second son became King Manuel II, but he was quite a young man and was unprepared to lead the country.

The republicans increased their attacks on the government. Together with the Carbonaria, a secret society of radicals led by Antonio Machado Dos Santos, they were mainly responsible for the overthrow of the government. These groups forced Manuel into exile and proclaimed the Republic of Portugal. Braga was named provisional president, and a constituent assembly was called to write a republican constitution.

Carlos I, King of Portugal. (*Library of Congress*)

The Republic Struggles

From the beginning, the Republic of Portugal was plagued by problems. The Republican Party split into factions—a moderate group led by Machado and a radical group that separated and became the Democratic Party, led by Afonso Costa, the Minister of Justice in the new government. Political fighting between the Democrats and moderate Republicans took up much time and energy that might otherwise have been given to reform.

With the support of his fellow ministers, Costa began a massive campaign against the clergy even before the Cortes Gerais (parliament) drafted a constitution. The church and state were separated, clerical property was put under the control of the state, the Jesuits were expelled, all monastic orders were dissolved, and the state was given full control of all education. After this first rush of activity to limit the power of the clergy, the Republicans decided to defend the Church—and by doing so caused tensions to increase.

In 1911, a constitution was drafted and promulgated. It was a fairly moderate document that set up a republican parliamentary system. Strikes by labor were permitted—a right that was immediately seized by working people across the country, who rallied to protest the government's lack of action to reform labor and the larger social system. Those who favored a return to monarchy also began to mount protests, and plots to reestablish a king caused the Republicans much concern during the early years of the Republic of Portugal.

Manuel José de Arriaga was named President of the Republic after the constitution was promulgated, but he was not able to provide political peace. The Portuguese people did not give wide support to their new form of government. In the first republican election in Lisbon, a city of 350,000 people, fewer than 20,000 voted. No party had a strong base of power. Costa's Democrats alternated in power with the Republicans, but the two parties gave most of their energy to debating whether the Church should be supported or further restricted, so that little attention was given to budget problems and needed social reforms.

Consequences

As the feud between the moderate Republicans and the Democrats prevented them from addressing any other issue but that of the Church's position, the army began to gain support as the only institution with enough prestige and respectability to keep the country from going out of control. In 1916, the Portuguese government joined the Allies in declaring war on Germany, and Portuguese troops were sent to the Western Front. Yet the Portuguese people had no real grudge against Germany, and the soldiers were not well prepared for war. Tensions within the country increased.

In December, 1917, Major Sidônio Bernardino Cardosa da Silva led the army in overthrowing the government and establishing a dictatorship. This desperate act still did not solve Portugal's problems, and da Silva was assassinated the following year.

BRITAIN'S PARLIAMENT PASSES THE NATIONAL INSURANCE ACT

With its provisions for health and unemployment insurance for manual laborers, the National Insurance Act of 1911 paved the way for the establishment of Great Britain's welfare state in the mid-1940's.

Laws for Social Reform

During the second half of the nineteenth century, the spread of the Industrial Revolution in Great Britain and the extension of voting rights combined to change British people's attitudes about the causes of and cures for poverty. Poverty came to be seen as the result of unemployment and other kinds of social and economic change caused by the ups and downs of various industries.

The Poor Law Administration, which up until this time had governed state aid to the poor in Great Britain, came under increasing attack, for it was seen as inadequate in dealing with poverty in an industrial nation. As the working class gained a political voice in the country, a "New Liberalism" developed at the beginning of the twentieth century, combining older Liberal thinking with socialism. A coalition of Liberal and Labour Members of Parliament was able to pass many laws for social reform between 1906 and 1911: the Old Age Pensions Act, the Labour Exchanges Act, the Trade Disputes Act, the Miners' Eight-Hour-Day Act, and the Trade Boards Act.

In 1906, before leaving office, the Conservative government had given a royal commission permission to study the Poor Law Administration to see how it should be reformed and updated. The commission also was to make recommendations about whether a state system of sickness insurance should be established.

Without waiting for the commission's final report, in 1908, David Lloyd George, Chancellor of the Exchequer, took a small group of officials

What: Social reform
When: May-December, 1911
Where: London
Who:
HERBERT HENRY ASQUITH (1852-1928), Liberal Prime Minister of Great Britain from 1908 to 1916
DAVID LLOYD GEORGE (1863-1945), Chancellor of the Exchequer from 1908 to 1915
WINSTON CHURCHILL (1874-1965), President of the Board of Trade from 1908 to 1910, and Home Secretary from 1910 to 1911

with him to tour Germany, where there was already a government program for meeting the health-care needs of the poor. Within a year, Lloyd George instructed Treasury officials to write a bill for social insurance. This bill was to set up a national, compulsory system of insurance, funded by contributions from the employee, the employer, and the state. It would make use of the "friendly societies" that already existed. Sponsored by fraternal organizations and labor unions, these societies sold sickness and accident insurance to more than six million Britons.

The Bill

In May, 1911, the National Health Insurance Bill was introduced in the House of Commons by the Liberal prime minister, Herbert Henry Asquith. It provided insurance benefits for all employed manual laborers, male and female, between the ages of sixteen and sixty-five, who earned less than 160 pounds per year. The sickness and medical benefits included ten shillings per week sickness pay, payment of doctors' fees, medicines, and special benefits such as thirty shillings for the expenses of pregnancy and delivery, and sanatorium treatment for those who suffered from tuberculosis. These benefits would be financed by fourpence deducted from the weekly pay of each employee, threepence per week contributed by employers for each employee, and twopence from the government for each employee.

The bill's second part set up a state system of unemployment insurance. Such a system had not been established by any other modern nation. This part of the bill was largely the work of Winston Churchill, who was President of the Board of Trade from 1908 to 1910, and William

Henry Beveridge, a young government worker who belonged to the Fabian Society, a socialist organization.

Because the bill was an experiment, and because insuring against industrial unemployment was risky, part 2 of the bill was at first restricted to building and engineering — trades in which employment was most subject to change. Like the sickness-insurance system, it was to be funded by compulsory contributions from the worker, the employer, and the government. The worker would be assured of receiving seven shillings per week as an unemployment payment for up to fifteen weeks.

The bill became controversial during long weeks of heated debate from May to December, 1911. The Labour Party was seeking more far-reaching changes — an extensive state-run institution to care for health needs, and laws to guarantee the right to work. The small "friendly

societies" feared interference by both the government and the large industrial insurance companies, which for political reasons Lloyd George had been forced to accept as "approved" societies.

It was British doctors, however, who raised the loudest objections. They were angry that Lloyd George planned to continue the "club practice," in which friendly societies contracted for the doctors' services. A "doctors' revolt" organized by the British Medical Association, an organization with quite a bit of political power, was finally ended when Lloyd George agreed to several of the doctors' demands: He approved free choices of doctors, the end of club practice, and increases in certain fees paid to the doctors.

In response to pressure from Scottish and Irish leaders, the plan was set up to be run by four independent "national insurance committees" for England, Ireland, Scotland, and Wales, but with a central National Health Insurance Joint Committee. In 1911, advocates for health insurance believed that this compromise was a mistake that would make the program ineffective.

With these various compromises and amendments, the National Insurance Act became law.

Consequences

The goal of the National Insurance Act of 1911 was to improve the living conditions of the working classes and, through a combination of government help and self-help, provide welfare services and income during periods of unemployment and sickness. The act was limited in its effectiveness: The insurance benefits were not generous, workers' families were not covered by the insurance, and hospital stays were not covered.

Yet the system was not designed to meet all the needs that existed, but to test whether such state-run social welfare programs could be made to work. The National Insurance Act created the first state-supported insurance in Great Britain, and it prepared the way for the much more extensive social welfare laws of the 1940's.

The English elections: an open-air reciting at the Portsmouth docks. (*Bain Collections, Library of Congress*)

Britain's Parliament Bill Limits the Power of the House of Lords

> Having reached deadlock over a national budget written by members of Great Britain's Liberal Party, the Houses of Parliament passed the Parliament Bill, which put strict limits on the House of Lords' power of veto.

What: Law and political reform
When: August 10, 1911
Where: London
Who:
HERBERT HENRY ASQUITH (1852-1928), Liberal Prime Minister of Great Britain from 1908 to 1916
DAVID LLOYD GEORGE (1863-1945), Chancellor of the Exchequer from 1908 to 1915
ARCHIBALD PHILIP PRIMROSE, EARL OF ROSEBERY (1847-1929), a Liberal leader in the House of Lords
HENRY CHARLES KEITH PETTY-FITZMAURICE, MARQUIS OF LANSDOWNE (1845-1927), a Conservative leader in the House of Lords
ARTHUR JAMES BALFOUR (1848-1930), a Conservative leader in the House of Commons
EDWARD VII (1841-1910), King of Great Britain from 1901 to 1910
GEORGE V (1865-1936), King of Great Britain from 1910 to 1936

The Budget Battle

The Liberal Party in Great Britain was the majority party in the House of Commons and was led by Herbert Henry Asquith, the prime minister. In 1909, however, though the Liberals had been elected by a landslide vote in 1906, they could not set up their program of new laws without interference or veto from the House of Lords, which was mostly Conservative. A number of important bills passed by the Commons had been thrown out by the Lords. Members of the House of Commons, being answerable to the voters, knew that something needed to change if they were to accomplish any real work.

In planning the national budget of 1909, Asquith and his cabinet faced the unpopular, but necessary, task of raising taxes and finding other sources of income for the government. An extra sixteen million pounds sterling were needed to pay old-age pensions; Great Britain needed to try to stay ahead of Germany in building warships; and the Liberals wanted to begin a new program of government aid to the poor.

David Lloyd George, Chancellor of the Exchequer, knew that the budget he had put together would upset many Conservatives. Taxes would be raised on liquor and tobacco, there would be new taxes on the sale of gasoline and cars, and income tax and death taxes would increase. The budget also proposed a new "supertax" on incomes over five thousand pounds and other new taxes on land and minerals. Many members of the House of Lords were wealthy landowners who would see these new taxes as a declaration of war against the rich by the Liberal government.

This "People's Budget" did lead to a long struggle between the Houses of Parliament in 1910 and 1911. From April to November, 1909, Parlia-

Election posters on the pavement in front of a polling place. (*Bain Collection, Library of Congress*)

ment was filled with debates on the budget. To go into effect, the budget would have to be passed not only by the House of Commons but also by the House of Lords — and the Lords were determined to exercise their veto. The Conservative leader of the House of Commons, Arthur James Balfour, led fellow Conservatives in opposing the budget without room for compromise. The whole country was engaged in the argument, and some Conservatives organized a Budget Protest League that drew thousands of supporters. Meanwhile, Lloyd George and his young aide Winston Churchill traveled throughout the country to criticize the House of Lords as an old-fashioned "rich men's club."

Many of the Lords believed the new budget to be unconstitutional. To pass it would be politically embarrassing to them, but if they rejected it, the Liberal government would dissolve and the question of the Lords' power of veto would become a political issue fought out at the polls. The Lords argued that in rejecting the budget, they were only exercising their ancient rights. The Liberals said that the budget was not included

among the Lords' ancient rights, and claimed that the Lords had not rejected a budget for more than 250 years.

Votes and Negotiations

On November 30, 1909, the Lords voted down the budget 350 to 75. The House of Commons immediately declared that the rejection of the budget was "a break of the Constitution and a usurpation of the rights of the Commons," and Asquith dissolved his cabinet.

Now matters were in the hands of the voters. In January, 1910, the Liberals were voted back into power. Though their majority in the House of Commons was not quite as large as before, Asquith was determined to keep the House of Lords from imposing its will. The powers of the Lords needed to be cut back if the Liberal program of social reform was to go forward.

In February, 1910, the government had introduced the Parliament Bill, which would severely restrict the Lords' power of veto. Under this bill, money bills would become law when passed by the House of Commons even without the consent

of the House of Lords. Other bills, if passed by the Commons in three consecutive sessions and rejected by the Lords, would become law if two years had passed between the first and third votes by the Commons. Also, the maximum life of a Parliament would be reduced from seven to five years.

As the battle over the Lords' powers began, the unexpected death of King Edward VII on May 6, 1910, suddenly silenced the arguments. The new king, George V, asked Asquith and Balfour to try to settle their differences in private conferences. They met privately many times during a six-month period but failed to resolve the deadlock, and when the debate returned to Parliament, Liberals and Conservatives were still in strong disagreement.

For the second time in less than a year, Asquith dissolved his cabinet and put the issue of the Lords' veto power directly before the voters. The Liberals again won a clear majority.

Now Asquith warned the Lords that if they rejected the Parliament Bill again, he would fill the House of Lords with new Liberal peers. By this threat, he revealed that King George V had promised to use his royal privileges to name as many new peers as necessary to pass the Parliament Bill through the House of Lords.

Ignoring the threat, the Lords insisted on amending the Parliament Bill. The Marquis of Lansdowne (Henry Charles Keith Petty-Fitzmaurice), the Lords' Conservative leader, then received a warning from Asquith: The amendments were unacceptable, and he was ready to ask the king to fulfill his promise to create new Liberal peers. Lansdowne backed down and persuaded the Lords to accept their defeat.

Consequences

The constitutional crisis ended on August 10, 1911, when the Parliament Bill squeezed through the House of Lords by 131 votes to 114, with most of the peers abstaining. Great Britain's government was now more fully in the hands of the people's elected representatives, rather than those who had inherited titles of nobility.

78

FRANCE AND GERMANY SIGN A TREATY ON MOROCCO

> *Long-standing conflicts over European interests in Morocco were finally resolved when Germany recognized France's protectorate over Morocco, but many Germans were unhappy with the compromise.*

A Long Dispute

In 1904, Great Britain and France formed an agreement called the Entente Cordiale. Great Britain received primary rights to establish its influence in Egypt, while France was given similar rights in Morocco. The French also persuaded Italy and Spain to agree to French supremacy in Morocco.

Leaders of Germany, however, were quite alarmed about this agreement. Germany had ambitions to spread its influence in North Africa as well, but France and Great Britain were not sympathetic to these ambitions.

The German response to the British and French agreement on dividing their influence in North Africa was led by Friedrich von Holstein, a politician who had been active in Germany's foreign affairs since the 1870's; in 1905 he became Undersecretary in the German Foreign Ministry. Following Holstein's plan, Kaiser William II set off to call on the Sultan of Morocco, and on March 31, 1905, in a bombastic speech in Tangier, he announced that Germany was interested in supporting a Moroccan move toward independence.

Chancellor Bernhard von Bülow then suggested publicly that Germany might go to war with France over Morocco. The Germans had decided that this threat was a safe one to make, for they believed that Russia, which was then at war with Japan, would not be able to come to France's aid, though Russia and France were allies under the terms of the Double Entente of 1894. France agreed to Germany's demand for an international conference to decide what was to be done about

What: International relations
When: November 4, 1911
Where: Morocco and Germany
Who:
WILLIAM II (1859-1941), Emperor of Germany from 1888 to 1918
PRINCE BERNHARD VON BÜLOW (1849-1929), Chancellor of Germany from 1900 to 1909
THEOBALD VON BETHMANN-HOLLWEG (1856-1921), Chancellor of Germany from 1909 to 1917
FRIEDRICH VON HOLSTEIN (1837-1909), Undersecretary of the German Foreign Ministry from 1905 to 1906
ALFRED VON KIDERLEN-WÄCHTER (1852-1912), German Foreign Secretary beginning in 1910

Morocco. The French people were angry that their leaders had given in to Germany on this matter, but Bülow was later made a prince for his handling of the situation.

The international conference was held at Algeciras, Spain, from January to April, 1906. At this conference, no other nation supported Germany's position. Even Austria-Hungary, Germany's partner in the Triple Alliance, was not interested in promoting German influence over Morocco. Spain was not very involved in the discussions, while Italy sided with France. Russia, no longer in the war with Japan, supported France, as did the United States. At the conference's end, the Act of

Algeciras upheld France's right to colonize Morocco, and the end result was that the alliance between France and Great Britain became all the stronger. The conference's effect had been opposite to what the Germans had intended, and as a result Undersecretary Holstein was fired by William II.

In 1907, discussions between Great Britain and Russia brought an end to the quarrels those two nations had had over control of certain regions of Asia. The Triple Entente of Great Britain, France, and Russia was growing up to stand against Germany. In 1909, Germany signed an agreement with France to divide their influence in Morocco: France would have a free hand in the north of that country, while Germany would be restricted to the south. France also promised to help Germany build a railroad from the German Cameroons to East Africa, across the French and Belgian Congos. Yet that help was never forthcoming.

Conflict and Compromise

Bülow resigned as chancellor in 1909, and was replaced by Theobald von Bethmann-Hollweg, who appointed Alfred von Kiderlen-Wächter as Foreign Secretary in the summer of 1910. It was Kiderlen-Wächter who handled the next Moroccan crisis, in 1911. He reasoned that the government needed to achieve some important success in colonization abroad, to distract the German people's attention from the growth of the Social Democratic Party in the German Reichstag, or parliament. Germany should seize a couple of ports in Morocco and insist that France agree to new terms there. William II approved the plan.

Because of uprisings in Morocco, the French moved into the interior of the country and occupied Fez on May 21, 1911. This intrusion contradicted the terms of the Algeciras agreement. Now Germany had its opportunity to assert equal claim to Morocco with France. The German gunboat *Panther* was sent to Agadir Harbor, and within Germany, the government started a campaign to make the Moroccan cause a popular one. Almost the whole country, except the Social Democrats, joined to call for German protection of Morocco's mineral ores.

Yet other European nations were even more opposed to German aims than they had been in 1905. Austria-Hungary did not come to its ally's aid. British Prime Minister David Lloyd George gave his famous Mansion House speech, promising that his nation would stand in solidarity with France over Morocco. In August, 1911, the British, Russians, and French met for discussions about possible military cooperation.

On July 15, 1911, Kiderlen-Wächter had demanded the whole of the French Congo (French Equatorial Africa with its capital, Brazzaville) in exchange for Germany's renunciation of all claims to Morocco. Two days later, the French prime minister rejected this demand. Meanwhile, Kaiser William II began to back down from Kiderlen-Wächter's threats. A council of advisers told him that war over Morocco would not be a good idea, since Germany was still trying to build up its navy, and since alliances among the other European powers were strong. William instructed Bethmann-Hollweg to bring about a negotiated settlement — a decision that was much attacked by certain business groups within Germany.

On November 4, 1911, representatives of France and Germany signed a treaty on Morocco. Germany recognized the French protectorate over Morocco and was allowed equal opportunity in that country. About 270,000 square kilometers in the French Congo, with more than a million inhabitants, were transferred to the German Cameroons.

Consequences

During the crisis, the people of Germany had, for the most part, become upset at what they saw as Germany's loss of power. Great Britain, which remained loyal to France, was criticized for trying to stop Germany's colonial and economic development. The Germans were not satisfied with the exchange of Morocco for land in central Africa, and many wanted war. Just after the signing of the treaty with France, there were furious debates in the Reichstag, and Bethmann-Hollweg and Kiderlen-Wächter were bitterly attacked.

In a speech on November 9, 1911, Bethmann-Hollweg defended his actions, arguing that Germany had won "free competition" in the Moroccan mines and had made secure its openings to the Congo and Ubangi rivers in central Africa. The treaty, he said, had improved relations between Germany and Great Britain.

Many German political parties and large sections of the press still were not satisfied. Insisting that Germany had been insulted by the outcome of the Moroccan affair, they called on Kaiser William and his government to prepare for war in the future. These attitudes among the German people were certainly a factor in the outbreak of World War I in 1914.

William II, German emperor. (*Library of Congress*)

ITALY ANNEXES TRIPOLI

In 1911-1912, Italy was successful in annexing Tripoli, which had been under Turkish control.

What: Military conflict
When: 1911-1912
Where: Tripoli and Cyrenaica (part of modern Libya)
Who:
GIOVANNI GIOLITTI (1842-1928), Prime Minister of Italy from 1911 to 1914
CARLO CANEVA (1845-1922), commander in chief of the Italian expeditionary force to Tripoli in 1911
ALBERTO POLLIO (1852-1914), Italian Chief of Staff
ALFRED VON KIDERLEN-WÄCHTER (1852-1912), German Foreign Secretary beginning in 1910
COUNT ALOIS LEXA VON AEHRENTHAL (1854-1912), Foreign Minister of Austria-Hungary from 1906 to 1912
COUNT FRANZ CONRAD VON HÖTZEN-DORF (1852-1925), Chief of Staff of the Austro-Hungarian army from 1906 to 1911 and from 1912 to 1917

The Italian Ambition

For thirty years, Italian leaders had been ambitious to establish an empire in North Africa. By 1902, Italy had obtained approval from Germany and Austria-Hungary, its partners in the Triple Alliance, and from France and Great Britain for an eventual move into Tripoli. Russia's approval was gained in 1909.

The Italians had several reasons for wanting to expand into North Africa. The reason they used most often was that their population was growing too large for their area, so that new territory was needed. In 1896, Italy had suffered an embarrassing disaster when it tried to conquer Ethiopia; one of its reasons for seeking to annex Tripoli, then, was its need to restore national pride and confidence. During the first decade of the twentieth century, Italy had been partially successful in making economic investments in Tripoli. When the Young Turks came to power in 1908, however, they put a stop to this economic advance.

By 1911, people throughout Italy were demanding that their fiftieth anniversary of national statehood be celebrated by the annexation of Tripoli. Giovanni Giolitti, the Liberal Prime Minister of Italy, saw no reasons to delay. In 1900, France had promised Italy a free hand in Tripoli, in exchange for Italy's approval of France's control over Morocco. France had achieved its goals in Morocco in 1911, when it had signed a treaty in which Germany had given up its rights to that country. Now Giolitti was ready to seize Tripoli as quickly as possible. The Italians believed that it was important to maintain a balance of power with the French in the Mediterranean area. They also feared that since Germany had been excluded from Morocco, the Germans would move to claim Tripolitan territories before Italy could do so.

War and Conquest

On September 28, 1911, Italy put a twenty-four-hour ultimatum before the sultan of the Ottoman Empire, threatening war because Turkey had supposedly mistreated Italian citizens and blocked Italian investments. Though the sultan tried to pacify the Italians, they declared war on the Ottoman Empire on September 29. On the first

Italian artillery outpost in the desert, Tripoli. (*Library of Congress*)

day of formal hostilities, Italy bombarded Turkish ports on the Tripolitan coast.

Alfred von Kiderlen-Wächter, Foreign Secretary of the German Empire, tried to mediate between the two states but had no success. On November 5, expecting a quick victory, Giolitti had King Victor Emmanuel III of Italy proclaim the formal annexation of all Libya. Yet this proclamation did not mean victory. The Turks fought well, carrying on the struggle for more than a year.

Italian Commander in Chief Carlo Caneva and Chief of Staff Alberto Pollio made three serious mistakes in conducting the war. First, they imagined that the Turks would give up quickly; second, they did not expect that the Arabs would ally themselves with the Turks; third, because they thought they would be waging a conventional war, they took only twenty thousand Italian troops to Tripoli.

Because the Turks used guerrilla strategies, Caneva and Pollio were forced to expand their forces to 100,000 men. Although the Italians did not gain a major victory in Africa, they did manage, in May, 1912, to capture Rhodes and other islands of the Dodecanese group in the Aegean Sea, previously held by Turkey.

It was not Italian strength but the threat of war with the Balkan States that finally forced the Turks to give up the struggle. Peace negotiations were opened in July, 1912. In the Treaty of Lausanne, signed on October 18, 1912, the Italians gained a certain amount of control over Libya, but that region officially remained under the rule of the Turkish sultan.

The Great Powers of Europe had various responses to Italy's war against the Ottoman Empire. Though all the major European states had at one time or another given their blessing to Italy's ambitions to take over Tripoli, several of them were not altogether pleased with the war. Russia, which had the most to gain from a weakening of

Turkey, was the only nation to give Italy full support. France supported Italy's action until January, 1912, when Italians boarded two French ships that they suspected of helping the Turkish war effort; after this incident, the French view of Italy's actions became less favorable. Great Britain expressed its concern that the war might lead to the complete collapse of Turkey and to Russia's taking complete control of the passageway between the Mediterranean and the Black Sea.

The strongest objections to Italy's war of conquest came from its allies, Germany and Austria-Hungary. William II, Emperor of Germany, feared that Italy's action might lead to a world war. The Foreign Minister of Austria-Hungary, Count Alois Lexa von Aehrenthal, announced that his government would not let Italy move its war against the Turks into the Balkans. Yet Aehrenthal stood against the demand by Austro-Hungarian Chief of Staff Count Franz Conrad von Hötzendorf that Austria declare war on Italy. When Conrad insisted, Emperor Francis Joseph I removed him temporarily of his command.

As the Tripolitan War was drawing to a close, the Balkan states of Serbia, Montenegro, Bulgaria, and Greece were preparing their own strike against the Ottoman Empire to try to gain more territory. The First Balkan War broke out in October, 1912.

Consequences

Italy's annexation of Tripoli proved to be a very costly action. Though the Italians felt proud of having gained a colony in Africa, this new colony was expensive to maintain and difficult to control. The Italians who were emigrating from their homeland preferred the United States to Tripoli, which was essentially a desert.

The conquest of Tripoli also altered politics within Italy. The moderate parties that had managed to control the government now gave way before the criticism of new nationalist groups, which demanded that Italy continue to make new conquests and spread its influence abroad. Demands such as these continued to be made loudly throughout Italy during and after World War I.

THE UNITED STATES ESTABLISHES A PUBLIC HEALTH SERVICE

What had begun as the Marine Hospital Service in 1798 grew to offer an increasing number of services to all Americans; in 1912, it was renamed the U.S. Public Health Service.

The Early Years

The United States Public Health Service has its origins in England in the sixteenth century, when the English people, out of gratitude for their navy's successes against the Spanish, established a seamen's hospital. Throughout much of the American Colonial period, the British government collected small taxes from its sailors to care for the sick and disabled.

After the United States was founded, Alexander Hamilton urged that a similar program be established; he reasoned that a good merchant marine was important for promoting American trade. In 1798, New York Congressman Edward Livingston pushed through Congress a bill that created the Marine Hospital Service. The law provided that the Treasury Department should collect twenty cents per month from each merchant seaman to support this service. The following year, the law was amended to include the navy and marines.

The first temporary U.S. Marine Hospital was established in Boston in 1799, and the first government-owned hospital was built in Norfolk County, Virginia. In 1802, the law was broadened to cover the crews on boats and rafts sailing down the Mississippi River to New Orleans. As the nation expanded toward the west, Congress, in 1837, provided for new hospitals in the Mississippi River Valley and the Great Lakes region.

During these years, the Marine Hospital Service was a responsibility of the Treasury Department, with local collectors of customs being assigned to oversee the collection of fees. Much of the medical care was provided on a contract basis,

What: Social reform
When: 1912
Where: Washington, D.C.
Who:
ALEXANDER HAMILTON (1757-1804), U.S. Secretary of the Treasury from 1789 to 1795
EDWARD LIVINGSTON (1764-1836), Congressman from New York from 1795 to 1801
JOHN M. WOODWORTH (fl. 1870), a surgeon

and the contracts were often handed out as political favors. The collector of customs was traditionally a political appointee as well. As a result, the quality of services patients received in the first seventy years of the Marine Hospital Service varied widely.

As the nineteenth century advanced, the service began to build more hospitals, but it became clear that their locations were chosen for political reasons. In New Orleans, work was started on a marine hospital in 1837. Delayed for many years, the project was finally completed in 1851 at a total cost of $123,000 — an enormous amount of money in those days. Though this building contract obviously had been mismanaged, an even larger hospital project was begun in 1855. This one was built in a swamp, and one of the walls sank two feet before the building was completed. This structure, which eventually cost half a million dollars, was never even used by the Marine Hospital Service.

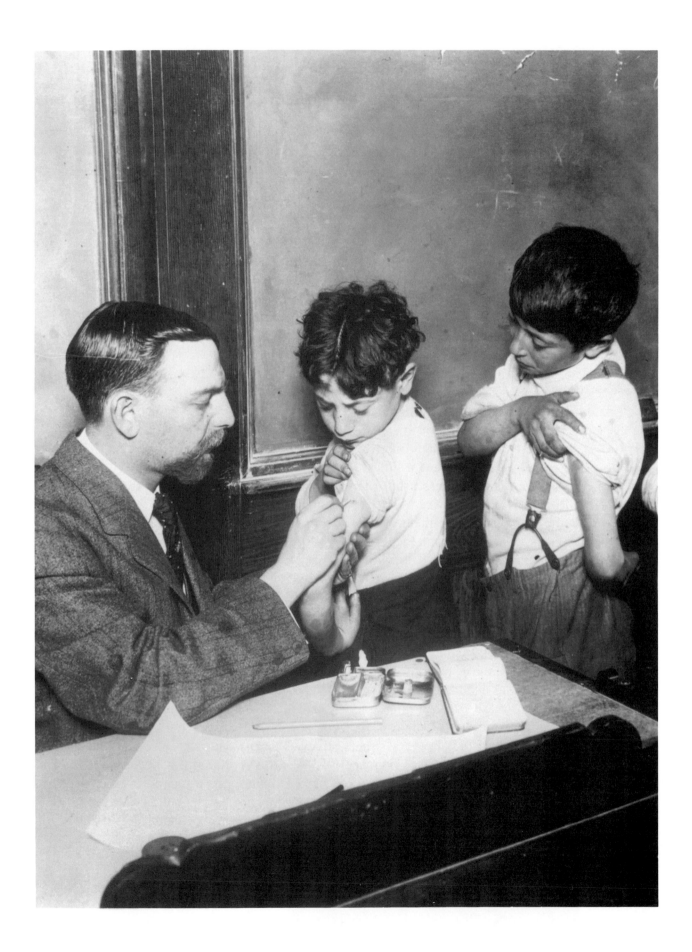

Reform and Growth

Because of complaints about the marine hospitals, Congress appointed a commission to investigate them in 1849. Seven years later, the commission's recommendations for improving procedures in the hospitals were put into effect. There was some improvement as a result, but political interference still kept most of the hospitals from providing the best health care at a low cost.

In 1870, Congress completely reorganized the Marine Hospital Service, making it a bureau of the Treasury Department, headed by a supervising surgeon. The first officer to hold this position was John M. Woodworth, a very able doctor and administrator. The law of 1870 also increased the hospital tax to forty cents per month. The monthly charge remained the same until 1884, when it was replaced with a tonnage tax. Finally, in 1906, the tonnage tax was replaced with direct appropriations by Congress.

Under Woodworth's leadership, the service improved dramatically. In 1873 he introduced a personnel policy by which health-service workers would be hired for their skill, not for political reasons. In this and other ways, he gradually raised the quality of the staff. The next advance came in 1889, when a commissioned-officer corps was created, giving the service a force of highly qualified health experts who could move around the country to help take care of specific needs and problems.

Woodworth was a supporter of the emerging public-health movement. He worked for a national quarantine system to help keep contagious diseases from spreading, and he helped draft the first federal quarantine law in 1878. After this law was passed, the Marine Hospital Service cooperated with state and city governments to improve their quarantine agencies. When Congress strengthened the National Quarantine Law in 1893, the Marine Hospital Service began taking over state and local quarantine stations, completing the work in 1921, when it took over the quarantine facilities of the Port of New York.

The responsibilities of the Marine Hospital Service were increased further by the Immigration Law of 1891, which required the service's medical officers to examine all immigrants. In 1887, a one-room bacteriological laboratory was set up in the Marine Hospital on Staten Island, New York. This laboratory was the forerunner of the Hygienic Laboratory for Bacteriological Research, which was established four years later in Washington, D.C.

Because of the growth and development of the Marine Hospital Service, Congress changed its name in 1902, to the United States Public Health and Marine Hospital Service. In 1912, the name was shortened to the United States Public Health Service.

Consequences

In the twentieth century, the U.S. Public Health Service has continued to provide new services. Its research laboratories have done outstanding work on epidemiology — the spread of diseases — and the service has played an important part in helping state and local health boards to work well. Under the Social Security Act of 1935, the Public Health Service was given responsibility for distributing eight million dollars each year for grants to public health agencies around the country. In the years since, the budget of the Public Health Service has increased dramatically.

The Public Health Service is now a division of the Department of Health, Education, and Welfare. It is headed by the U.S. surgeon general, and its divisions include the National Library of Medicine, the Bureau of State Services, the Bureau of Medical Services, and the National Institutes of Health.

Schoolchildren being vaccinated, 1910. (*National Archives*)

THE MANCHU DYNASTY IS OVERTHROWN IN THE CHINESE REVOLUTION

> *The Chinese Revolution of 1911 succeeded in ousting the Manchu Dynasty, but revolutionary leaders were not able to unify China.*

What: Political reform
When: February 12, 1912
Where: China
Who:

SUN YAT-SEN (1866-1925), a Chinese revolutionary leader who conspired against the Manchus

TZ'U-HSI (1835-1908), Dowager Empress of China from 1861 to 1908

HUANG HSING (1873-1916), a Chinese revolutionary conspirator who cooperated with Sun Yat-sen

CH'UN (1883-1951), Prince Regent of China from 1908 to 1912

HENRY P'U-YI (1906-1967), the last Manchu Emperor of China, from 1908 to 1912

YÜAN SHIH-K'AI (1859-1916), a military officer under the Manchus, and President of China from 1912 to 1916

Call for Reform

The most important cause of the Chinese Revolution of 1911 was the impact of Western nations on China. Ever since the disastrous Opium War of 1839-1842, the Chinese, who had long believed their civilization to be far superior to all others, had watched helplessly as other nations chipped away at their sovereignty. These other nations included not only the Great Powers of the West but, after 1895, Japan as well. Intent on gaining special trade privileges, these nations were caught up in a fierce rivalry. Their competition at least had the benefit of keeping China from becoming the colony of any single European state. The Manchu Dynasty, established in the seventeenth century, seemed unable to respond to the foreign threats.

After China was defeated in the Sino-Japanese War of 1895, the Chinese people rose up against foreign influences in the Boxer Rebellion. Yet, in 1900, a multinational army assembled by the Great Powers was able to defeat this revolt. After this humiliation, thoughtful Chinese increasingly began calling for an end to the ineffective Manchu leadership. Some young revolutionaries said that the monarchy must be altogether abolished in order to save China. One of the earliest and most prominent of these revolutionaries was Sun Yat-sen.

Born in the southern Chinese province of Kwangtung in 1866, Sun had emigrated to Hawaii as a teenager. There he had received a Western education and had been converted to Christianity. Although Sun wanted China to be strong enough to stand against Western imperialism, he also wanted to see the nation copy what he saw as the good aspects of modern Western civilization.

In October, 1895, Sun and a group of fellow revolutionaries, using Hong Kong as a base, tried to begin a rebellion in Canton, the capital of Kwangtung Province. When this rebellion was defeated, Sun was forced to leave China. He then spent long years as a political exile in Japan, Southeast Asia, and the West.

Sun Yat-sen. (*National Archives*)

In the summer of 1905, Sun Yat-sen, Huang Hsing (another anti-Manchu exile), and others founded the Revolutionary Alliance, or T'ung-Meng-hui. This revolutionary coalition, led by Sun, brought together all the foes of the Manchu regime. Overseas Chinese (Chinese people who had emigrated to Southeast Asia, and their descendants) began to give financial support to the coalition. Until 1911, however, all Sun's schemes for stirring up revolt in China came to nothing.

After 1900, Manchu Dowager Empress Tz'u-hsi, who had once strongly opposed reform, suddenly had a change of heart. There were many changes in the government during the first decade of the twentieth century. Locally elected provincial assemblies were established, and a constitutional parliamentary government was promised for the future. Public officials began to be selected on the basis of their training in specific skills rather than on the basis of their knowledge of the Confucian classics. A new educational system was established to train leaders, and certain students were sent abroad for further training. Also, the army was modernized and made more efficient.

Yet all these changes did not make the Chinese people more content with the rule of the Manchus. Instead, dissent increased. The new standards for

總理遺像

the selection of government officials actually made it harder for poor or middle-class young men to find a place in government bureaucracy, since more schooling was now required, and education was expensive. Instead, many of these ambitious young men entered the army, where they continued to oppose the Manchu regime. In the new schools and colleges, students developed a questioning, rebellious attitude toward the Manchus. Similarly, the provincial assemblies became places where local leaders could push for a greater say in running their own affairs.

Uprising and Revolution

After the dowager empress' death in 1908, there was no strong ruler able to keep a lid on the boiling pot of discontent. The year 1911 was marked by famine, floods, and economic disaster. In May of that year, Prince Regent Ch'un, who governed in the name of the "boy emperor" P'u-yi, became quite unpopular because he delayed calling a parliament, created a cabinet made up mostly of Manchus, and tried to get a foreign loan to pay for his plan to nationalize the railways. Protests arose in various parts of China. Normally, the army would have been able to crush dissent, but rebellion was beginning to spread within its ranks as well.

In October, a revolutionary organization was founded in the garrison of Wuchang, capital of the province of Hubei. Instead of submitting to discipline, the soldiers revolted on October 10, kidnapped their commander, and forced him, under threat of death, to lead their rebellion against the Manchu Dynasty. This day became known as the "Double Ten" among Chinese patriots.

Across the nation, the response to this mutiny was sudden and strong. Assembly after assembly in the provinces declared independence from the Manchu Dynasty. Soon a revolutionary regime was established in the central Chinese city of Nanking. All that remained for the Manchus was the capital city, Peking, and several provinces in northern China.

Sun Yat-sen returned from exile in December, and on December 29, 1911, he was elected Provisional President of the Republic of China by the Nanking government.

Yet the revolutionary victory was not complete. Yüan Shih-k'ai, an able military leader, had come out of retirement to defend the Manchus. His forces were far too strong for Nanking to defeat, but far too weak to defeat the new Nanking government. After some bargaining, the ambitious Yüan struck a deal with the revolutionaries. Yüan would persuade the Manchus to abdicate; in return, he would become President of China.

On February 12, 1912, the Manchus formally announced the end of their dynasty. Three days later, Sun Yat-sen resigned the presidency, recommending that Yüan be named as his successor. On March 10, 1912, Yüan Shih-k'ai was formally sworn in as Provisional President of the Republic of China. In response to his urging, the provisional parliament voted on April 1 to transfer the capital to Peking. China was now a united republic.

Consequences

The revolution did not secure liberal democracy in China. On March 20, 1913, Sung Chiao-jen, a liberal who had drafted the new constitution, was assassinated. In July and August, Yüan took power away from the provinces and banned all organized opposition to his regime. Sun Yat-sen was once again forced into exile in Japan.

After Yüan died in June, 1916, China soon disintegrated into a number of feuding states ruled by warlords. Sun died in 1925, and internal peace did not come to China until 1949, when the Communists, led by Mao Tse-tung, secured power over the mainland, while the Nationalists, led by Chiang Kai-shek, were confined to the island of Taiwan. Both the Communist regime and the Nationalist government claimed to be the exclusive heir to the glorious tradition of Sun Yat-sen and the Chinese Revolution of 1911.

HOME RULE STIRS DEBATE IN IRELAND AND BRITAIN

As Irish nationalists pressed for the reestablishment of the Irish Parliament, the issue of Ireland's ties to the rest of Great Britain became so controversial that the United Kingdom nearly broke out in civil war.

The Drive for Home Rule

The Act of Union of 1800, which established the United Kingdom of Great Britain and Ireland, had never been popular in Ireland. Throughout the nineteenth century, many Irish people had called for the restoration of the Irish Parliament, or Home Rule. The issue became important in British politics in the 1880's, when the Irish Members of Parliament, led by Charles Stewart Parnell, used their eighty-five votes to keep the Liberals in power, in exchange for Home Rule.

As a result, William Ewart Gladstone's Liberal government introduced the First Home Rule Bill in 1886, but it was defeated by thirty votes, and part of the Liberal Party, the Liberal Unionists (who opposed Home Rule), broke away. Gladstone's Second Home Rule Bill passed the House of Commons by thirty-four votes in 1893, but it was soundly defeated in the House of Lords by a vote of 419 to 41.

In the following years, the Conservative and Unionist governments of Great Britain tried to distract the Irish from the issue of Home Rule by making economic reforms to benefit the Irish. John Edward Redmond, an eloquent speaker, became leader of the united Irish Nationalist Party in the House of Commons in 1900. Yet since neither the Liberals nor the Conservatives needed Irish votes at that time, no progress was made until 1910. In the campaign of that year, the Liberals supported Home Rule. They lost so many seats in Parliament that they needed the votes of the Irish Nationalists to form a cabinet and ensure that their proposed program could go forward.

What: Political reform
When: April 11, 1912-September 15, 1914
Where: London and Ireland
Who:
HERBERT HENRY ASQUITH (1852-1928), Liberal Prime Minister of Great Britain from 1908 to 1916
WINSTON CHURCHILL (1874-1965), First Lord of the Admiralty from 1911 to 1915, and Liberal leader in the House of Commons
BONAR LAW (1858-1923), Conservative leader in the House of Commons
JOHN EDWARD REDMOND (1856-1918), leader of the Irish Nationalist Party
EDWARD HENRY CARSON (1854-1935), leader of the Ulster Unionists
EOIN MACNEILL (1867-1945), founder of the Nationalist Volunteers and leader of the Gaelic League
PADHRAIC PEARSE (1879-1916), leader of the Irish Republicans (Sinn Féin)

Now that they needed the help of the Irish Nationalists, the Liberals were obligated to put together a new Home Rule bill. The House of Lords would no longer be an obstacle, since the Parliament Act of 1911 had reduced its power.

Debate over the Bill

The Third Home Rule Bill was introduced into the House of Commons on April 11, 1912, by the

Liberal prime minister, Herbert Henry Asquith. The bill was managed by the First Lord of the Admiralty, Winston Churchill, who was then Liberal leader in the House of Commons and a strong supporter of Home Rule. Like the two previous Home Rule bills, this one would set up an Irish Parliament in Dublin, but control over foreign affairs, customs duties, and defense would remain with the British Parliament at Westminster. The number of Irish Members of Parliament at Westminster was to be reduced by half, to forty-two.

Redmond and the Irish Nationalists praised the bill and argued that it would strengthen the relationship between Great Britain and Ireland. The Liberal leaders praised it as a way of providing justice and greater independence for Ireland. Another Liberal argument was that Home Rule would relieve the British Parliament of the burden of having to deal with local affairs in Ireland.

Yet the Unionists—both the Conservative Unionists, led by Bonar Law, and the Ulster Unionists, led by Edward Henry Carson— opposed the Home Rule Bill bitterly. Their chief concern was the fate of Ulster, present-day Northern Ireland. The mostly Protestant Scottish-Irish residents of Ulster saw themselves as loyal Britons who were being sacrificed to the interests of the Roman Catholic residents of Southern Ireland, which was more rural. They were convinced that the Catholic Irish would persecute them religiously and economically.

Neither the North nor the South wished to divide Ireland into two separate states. There was a small but influential Protestant minority in the South, and the Ulster Protestants did not want to abandon them to the domination of Catholics. The

Irish Nationalists—predominately Catholics—wanted Ireland to remain one nation.

After vigorous debate, the Home Rule Bill passed the House of Commons on January 16, 1913. As had been expected, the House of Lords rejected it by a huge majority, which meant that the bill would have to be passed again by the Commons at its next two sessions to overcome the Lords' veto. Because the same Parliament would still be in session at that time, however, it was almost certain to pass.

Carson began to call on fellow Ulsterites to rise up against Great Britain. At first, the Liberal government did not take this threat too seriously. Then, however, a "covenant" opposing Home Rule gained a total of 470,000 signatures, and the Ulster Unionists began to drill a militia, the Ulster Volunteers. Conservative leaders gave open support to this threatened rebellion.

The Southern Irish were quite upset by Ulster's defiance and British weakness in the face of these threats. While Redmond continued to support Asquith and Parliament, other Irish people became convinced of the need for stronger measures than Home Rule. Groups such as the Irish Republicans, or Sinn Féin, the Gaelic League, and certain labor unions urged the South to arm itself just as Ulster had. In November, 1913, the Nationalist Volunteers, led by Eoin MacNeill and by Padhraic Pearse, leader of the Sinn Féin, began to drill in the South.

Because of these threats, when the Home Rule Bill passed the Commons for the third and last time in March, 1914, Asquith added an Amending Bill. This compromise excluded Ulster from Home Rule for six years. Redmond reluctantly accepted it, but the radical Irish Nationalist groups objected.

Meanwhile, German rifles were smuggled into Ulster for the Ulster Volunteers. The Nationalist Volunteers in the South were also growing in influence and becoming restless. Redmond unwillingly took command of them in May to keep his ties with MacNeill, Pearse, and Sir Roger David Casement, a rebel who was later hanged as a traitor.

The Home Rule Bill passed the Commons on May 25, and the Amending Act passed the Commons on June 23. The House of Lords then amended the Amending Act enough to destroy the compromise Asquith had worked out. On July 12, Carson proclaimed the establishment of the "Ulster Provisional Government."

Negotiations were not working, and on July 26, British troops fired on an angry crowd in Bachelors' Walk, Dublin. Three people were killed and many others wounded. The Irish Nationalists became even angrier, and civil war seemed about to begin.

The next day, however, Austria declared war on Serbia, and by August 4, Great Britain was plunged into World War I. In this crisis, Asquith, Redmond, Carson, and Law agreed to postpone the Amending bill, and the threat of civil war passed. On September 15, the Home Rule Bill became law, but Parliament agreed not to put it into effect until after the war.

Consequences

With the outbreak of World War I, Home Rule was no longer a real possibility. The radical Irish Nationalists soon split from Redmond to gain more followers. Eventually they were responsible for the Easter Rebellion of 1916 and for civil war after 1918.

The battle over the Home Rule Bill had many serious consequences for England and Ireland. The Conservatives' preaching of revolution had seriously threatened Great Britain's parliamentary system of government. The failure to enforce Home Rule helped to break the bonds between Great Britain and Ireland, preparing the way for the Irish Rebellion and eventual independence. Furthermore, Ulster opposition to Home Rule helped to cause the permanent split of Northern Ireland from the rest of the island.

Bonar Law (*AP/Wide World Photos*)

U.S. Marines Are Sent to Nicaragua to Quell Unrest

> By sending marines into Nicaragua, the United States prevented the Nicaraguan people from choosing their own government.

What: Political aggression
When: August 3, 1912
Where: Nicaragua
Who:
José Santos Zelaya (1845-1919), dictator of Nicaragua from 1893 to 1909
General Juan J. Estrada (1871-1947), leader of the 1909 revolt that overthrew Zelaya
Adolfo Díaz (1874-1964), President of Nicaragua from 1913 to 1917 and from 1926 to 1928
Augusto César Sandino (1895-1934), a legendary guerrilla leader
Anastasio Somoza García (1896-1956), dictator of Nicaragua from 1936 to 1956

Rebellion in Nicaragua

In the nineteenth century, political leaders struggled to gain control of Nicaragua, and there were many abuses of human rights: election fraud, political corruption, destruction and confiscation of property, exile, execution, and murder. These problems decreased toward the end of the century, as José Santos Zelaya began to gain power.

Zelaya was a dictator, but he was also a Liberal who expanded education, improved the armed forces, and encouraged trade. Still, the United States was not pleased with his rule. At the beginning of the twentieth century, American leaders began planning to build a canal across Central America, and Nicaragua was their first choice of location. Zelaya eagerly wanted a canal, but he insisted that Nicaragua's sovereignty must be guarded. As a result, the Americans decided to construct a canal through Panama instead.

Along with many other Nicaraguans, Zelaya resented this loss and hoped that another world power would decide to build a canal through Nicaragua. In angry public speeches, he pushed for a canal agreement with Germany and Japan. This possibility was alarming to American leaders, for they were determined to keep European powers out of the Americas.

On October 10, 1909, a revolt against Zelaya broke out in the Atlantic port of Bluefields. This uprising was led by General Juan J. Estrada, who was governor over the Atlantic coastal region of Nicaragua. Soon Zelaya's forces caught two American mercenaries laying mines in the San Juan River. These two men were quickly tried, condemned, and executed by a firing squad.

Though these two soldiers had become officers in the revolutionary movement and in doing so had given up their rights as American citizens, the United States took the opportunity to break diplomatic relations with Zelaya's government. On December 1, 1909, Zelaya resigned and went into exile.

The Americans Interfere

The United States had already sent gunboats to the Bluefields area, and after the revolution began American Marines had landed in Nicaragua, supposedly to protect American lives and

Scene at a dock in Nicaragua awaiting the arrival of U.S. Marines. (*Library of Congress*)

property. Declaring Bluefields a neutral zone, the United States kept the Nicaraguan government forces from shelling the revolutionaries. Since the revolutionaries had control of the port, they were able to receive customs money as well as weapons shipments from abroad.

The Nicaraguan congress chose José Madriz, a respected Liberal judge, to replace Zelaya, but the United States refused to recognize him. Though the Liberals were a majority in Nicaragua, the United States insisted that the Conservatives were the true representatives of the people.

In 1910, the United States supported Estrada as Provisional President of Nicaragua. He put together a government that included both Liberals and Conservatives, but when the marines left, the coalition fell apart. In May, 1911, Estrada resigned and gave his place to the vice president, Adolfo Díaz (another Conservative).

When the Liberals, led by Benjamín Zeledón, revolted, Díaz asked for U.S. help. On August 3, 1912, twenty-seven hundred U.S. Marines landed and took over the main railroad and principal cities. The Conservatives quickly hunted down the Liberal leaders and displayed Zeledón's body as a prize.

For almost all the next twenty years, U.S. Marines would stay in Nicaragua. Usually there were not more than one hundred at a time, but that was enough to keep the peace and protect the political leaders whom the United States wished to support.

The United States also became deeply involved in Nicaragua's finances. After Zelaya fell in 1909, the country's finances had become chaotic, with many debts to foreign creditors. To prevent European countries from moving into Nicaragua to recover the money that was owed to them, the United States arranged for new loans from New York bankers. To pay back the new loans, however, Nicaragua had to mortgage its future customs duties and its income from rail and steamship transportation. American bankers set up the National Bank of Nicaragua, whose board of

directors met in New York City rather than in Nicaragua.

In the Bryan-Chamorro Treaty, which was signed in 1914 and ratified in 1916, the United States bought the right to construct a canal through Nicaragua for only three million dollars. Having finished the Panama Canal in 1914, the United States had no intention of building another in Nicaragua; the only purpose of the treaty was to prevent any other world power from building a Central American canal.

Consequences

Realizing that the Nicaraguans were not happy with U.S. interference in their affairs, the United States withdrew the marines in 1925 and trained the Nicaraguan National Guard as a replacement. A new government of Conservatives and Liberals was formed, but the Conservatives were not cooperative, and the Liberals soon rebelled again. U.S. Marines returned to Nicaragua in 1926; by the next February, there were fifty-four hundred marines and eleven destroyers and cruisers in Nicaraguan cities and ports.

Finally, the United States tried to come to an agreement with the Liberals — but one Liberal general, Augusto César Sandino, had had enough. He demanded that the United States leave Nicaragua immediately and let it solve its own problems. The National Guard tried to hunt Sandino down, but he and his supporters used guerrilla warfare to escape capture.

For six years, the United States had two thousand soldiers fighting Sandino and helping the National Guard. Bombs were dropped on Nicaraguan villages, killing many civilians, but Sandino and his movement endured. Finally the United States pulled the marines out in January, 1933, leaving behind Anastasio Somoza García as head of the National Guard.

Somoza found a way to assassinate Sandino on February 23, 1934, and with the support of the National Guard Somoza became President of Nicaragua in 1936. Until his own assassination in 1956, he ruled Nicaragua as a dictator, using beatings, torture, imprisonment, and murder against his opponents. After his death, his two sons took power and carried on the tradition of dictatorship. Educated in the United States, the younger Somozas kept close ties with the American government.

In 1961, the Sandinista Front of National Liberation (FSLN), named in Sandino's honor, was founded and began an eighteen-year guerrilla struggle against the Somozas. On July 19, 1979, the last Somoza was brought down and the Sandinistas took power in Nicaragua.

THE BALKAN WARS DIVIDE EUROPEAN LOYALTIES

> *Two wars fought in southeastern Europe increased tensions among the various European states and set the stage for the eruption of World War I.*

The First War

Since 1908, when Austria had annexed the Turkish provinces of Bosnia and Hercegovina, Russia had wanted to keep Austria from advancing any farther in the Balkans, especially against Serbia. So from 1909 to 1913, Russia worked for the establishment of a Balkan League, based on separate agreements between Bulgaria on the one hand and Serbia, Greece, and Montenegro on the other, along with an accord between Montenegro and Serbia.

The league finally came into existence in 1912, but the leaders of its various nations were not interested in simply maintaining things as they were in the Balkans in order to please Russia. Austria's annexation of Bosnia and Hercegovina in 1908 and Italy's annexation of Tripoli in 1912 encouraged the members of the Balkan League to try to drive the Turks out of Europe altogether and divide the conquered lands among themselves.

None of the Great Powers wanted to see such a war, which might easily spread beyond the Balkans. Austria and Russia were particularly concerned. On October 8, 1912, Foreign Minister Count Leopold von Berchtold of Austria-Hungary and Russian Minister of Foreign Affairs Sergei Dmitrievich Sazonov, speaking for all the European powers, made a declaration to the Balkan States warning them not to make war on the Turks. The declaration warned that if the Balkan nations did make war and won (a possibility that was considered very unlikely), they would not be allowed to annex any territory.

Yet the warning came too late. On the same day it was issued, Montenegro boldly declared war on

What: Military conflict
When: October 18, 1912
Where: The Balkans
Who:
COUNT LEOPOLD VON BERCHTOLD (1863- 1942), Foreign Minister of Austria-Hungary from 1912 to 1915
SERGEI DMITRIEVICH SAZONOV (1861- 1927), Russian Minister of Foreign Affairs from 1910 to 1916
SIR EDWARD GREY (1862-1933), Foreign Secretary of Great Britain from 1905 to 1916
FERDINAND I OF SAXE-COBURG (1861- 1948), King of Bulgaria from 1908 to 1918

the Ottoman Empire. War began in earnest on October 18, when Bulgaria, Serbia, and Greece entered the conflict.

Six weeks later, on December 3, the badly beaten Turks called for an armistice. At the same time, a serious international crisis had arisen over Serbia's occupation of a stretch of the northern Adriatic coast of Albania. Austria and Italy were completely opposed to Serbia's taking control of any part of the Adriatic coastline, for that would allow Serbia and Russia to challenge the naval supremacy of the Austrians and Italians. Rather reluctantly, Germany agreed to support Austria if Austria were attacked while defending its interests.

Sazonov, afraid that Austria might pose a threat to Serbian interests (as had happened in 1908), spoke up for Serbian claims. Realizing, however, that Russia was not yet ready to become involved in a major war, Sazonov worked to resolve the conflict through negotiation. He helped to organize the London Peace Conference, which opened on December 16, 1912, under the chairmanship of Edward Grey, Foreign Secretary of Great Britain.

Early in 1913, Austria and Italy were able to gain some acceptance from other European powers for the creation of an enlarged Albania, which would safely keep Serbia from having access to the Adriatic. Meanwhile, hostilities had broken out again between members of the Balkan League and the Turks, on January 30, 1913. The Turks, however, were again defeated, and the Treaty of London of May 30, 1913, brought the First Balkan War to a close.

The Second War

None of the Balkan States was satisfied, however, with the terms it had been forced to accept in

London. Because Serbia had been denied an outlet to the Adriatic, it demanded a substitute: Bulgaria should give it a larger slice of Macedonian territory than the Treaty of London had assigned. Bulgaria indignantly refused. Bulgaria also did not want to give in to Greece's claims to the Thessalonica area of Macedonia or Romania's claims to the Dobruja, an area near the mouth of the Danube River.

Surrounded by hostile nations, Ferdinand I of Saxe-Coburg, who had been the independent King of Bulgaria since 1908, decided to remove the Serbs and the Greeks from Macedonia. Bulgaria attacked on June 29, 1913, and in response Serbia and Greece declared war on Bulgaria. They were soon joined by Montenegro and Romania, and then by their former enemy, the Ottoman Empire.

Bulgaria suffered a serious defeat. On August 10 in Bucharest, it agreed to terms of peace with the Balkan States and gave back the territories it

had wanted to take over. In a separate peace treaty with Turkey, signed at Constantinople on September 29, Bulgaria gave Turkey the greater part of Thrace (which it had gained in the First Balkan War), including the important city of Adrianople.

Consequences

The Balkan Wars were over, but the peace of southeastern Europe was in ruins, and the stability of all Europe remained in danger. Relations between Austria and Serbia became even more bitter. The combined might of Austria-Hungary and Germany had, once again, forced Russia to back down in its support of Serbia. This was quite humiliating for Russia. Bulgaria and Turkey were dissatisfied with the results of the Balkan Wars; when World War I broke out, these two nations ended up joining forces with Austria-Hungary and Germany.

Montenegro: an outpost of the Malissori. (*Library of Congress*)

WILSON IS ELECTED TO THE U.S. PRESIDENCY

> *With the Republican Party split between two candidates, Democrat Woodrow Wilson won the U.S. presidency and brought a new era of social and political reform.*

What: National politics
When: November, 1912
Where: The United States
Who:
WOODROW WILSON (1856-1924), President of the United States from 1913 to 1921
WILLIAM HOWARD TAFT (1857-1930), President of the United States from 1909 to 1913
THEODORE ROOSEVELT (1858-1919), President of the United States from 1901 to 1909, and leader of the new Progressive Party
JAMES BEAUCHAMP "CHAMP" CLARK (1850-1921), Speaker of the House of Representatives from Missouri from 1911 to 1919
OSCAR UNDERWOOD (1862-1929), an influential congressman from Alabama
LOUIS DEMBITZ BRANDEIS (1856-1941), a lawyer who later became a member of the Supreme Court

The Republican Disaster

When Theodore Roosevelt left the United States presidency in 1909, he was succeeded by William Howard Taft. Taft, who had been supported by Roosevelt, was expected to continue Roosevelt's progressive reforms. Roosevelt went off to Africa on a hunting expedition, believing that the White House would continue to operate much as it had during his presidency.

Through Roosevelt's ability to negotiate and to compromise between liberal and conservative policies, he had been able to hold together an unusual balance of supporters in Congress, including Eastern conservatives and Midwestern and urban progressives. Taft lacked both the physical energy and the political know-how to keep this coalition of support operating. He was a conservative at heart and, unable to inspire a commitment to unity, let the Republican Party fall apart into squabbling factions.

When Roosevelt returned home in 1910, the party was in a state of disarray, and the Democrats had scored important gains in the local and congressional elections of that year. By 1912, the division among Republicans had become even greater. Roosevelt marched out of the Republican convention in Chicago on June 22, 1912, to form the new Progressive Party. With this split in Republican loyalties, the election of a Democrat to the presidency was almost certain.

Wilson Campaigns and Wins

When the Democrats gathered in Baltimore on June 25, 1912, the party was at historic crossroads. Woodrow Wilson had been the front-runner for the presidential nomination until the Republican split made the Democratic nomination much more valuable. The new leader for the nomination was Champ Clark, the Speaker of the House. He was a typical old-line politician who had broadened his base of support from his home state of Missouri to attract many in the West who had at one time supported William Jennings

Woodrow Wilson. (*White House Historical Association*)

Bryan. Another leading candidate, Oscar Underwood of Alabama, had strong backing in the South. After a bitter convention fight, on the forty-sixth ballot Wilson finally won the nomination.

Wilson had campaigned for and won his first political office, the governorship of New Jersey, only in 1910. Before his entrance into politics, Wilson had had a career as a respected scholar. He had been graduated from Princeton University in 1879 and had practiced law for a short time; then he finished a doctorate in political science and history at The Johns Hopkins University in 1886. In 1902, he had been elected president of Princeton University. By that time, he had already written three books on the American system of government.

Some of his educational reforms eventually led to a dispute at Princeton, and just at that time (1910) he had the opportunity to enter politics as a candidate for the governorship of New Jersey. As governor, Wilson began certain basic reforms that changed New Jersey's government from a corrupt regime run by political bosses into a reform-oriented state. His successes had brought him to national attention as a leader in the Democratic Party.

The election became a confrontation between two progressive philosophies that reflected the new realities of an industrial society. Roosevelt's New Nationalism argued for a strong federal government. Roosevelt wanted to strengthen and regulate large corporations and to launch a program of government-supported social welfare.

In responding, Wilson obtained the help of a prominent Massachusetts lawyer, Louis D. Brandeis. Wilson's New Freedom platform emphasized giving power to state and local governments, breaking up large corporations, and encouraging small businesses.

In the election, Wilson won with 6,293,454 votes to Roosevelt's 4,119,538, Taft's 3,484,980, and Socialist Eugene V. Debs' 900,672. Even though Wilson's share of the popular vote was only 42 percent, he won an overwhelming victory in the electoral college, with 435 votes to Roosevelt's 88 and Taft's 8.

Consequences

As a newcomer in politics, Woodrow Wilson was not burdened with political debts like the favors Roosevelt owed to Eastern Republican business interests. Wilson also was fortunate to deal with a sympathetic Congress that was ready to cooperate in bringing about progressive reforms.

Wilson strengthened the presidency even further than Roosevelt had. He became the leader of the people as well as the Congress, and he dominated the government in both his terms. In his first term he influenced Congress to pass important legislative reforms in tariffs and banking and the breaking up of business monopolies. Later he added to his own program almost all the proposals Roosevelt had championed in the great debate of 1912. When the United States was drawn into World War I, Wilson became the first of the powerful war presidents of the twentieth century.

The effects of the 1912 campaign and of Wilson's election to the presidency have continued in American liberal politics. The New Deal of Franklin D. Roosevelt contained many echoes of Wilson's thinking, and the expansion of power Wilson brought about for the executive branch allowed the later programs of social welfare to be carried out. In international affairs, Wilson's Fourteen Points, which promised a peace without victory in World War I, expressed some of the ideals that are still being debated in American foreign policy.

THE SIXTEENTH AMENDMENT LEGALIZES THE INCOME TAX

With the passing of the Sixteenth Amendment to the Constitution, Congress gained the power to collect taxes on incomes, without apportionment among the states and without regard to the census.

The Tax Question

The history of income tax in the United States dates back to the War of 1812, when Secretary of the Treasury Alexander J. Dallas recommended on January 21, 1815, that Congress adopt a tax on incomes to raise funds for waging the war. Although the war had been ended with the signing of the Treaty of Ghent on December 24, 1814, this fact was probably not yet known in Washington in January, 1815. Once it was known that the war was over, however, Congress did not act on Secretary Dallas' request.

The income-tax question did not arise again until the Civil War, when the United States' first income tax was levied by the Union government. The Internal Revenue Act of 1862 provided for a tax on incomes and also said that this tax would be progressive — that is, the rates would be higher on higher incomes. For the first time in American history, people were to be taxed according to their ability to pay. The Act of 1862 called for a 3 percent tax on incomes up to ten thousand dollars and a 5 percent tax on incomes over that amount. The income tax remained in effect — though the rates changed — until 1872, when Congress let the law expire because of pressure from business groups.

In the late 1880's, however, the Populists and other groups began to call for a new income tax. In fact, the national platform of the Populist Party in 1892 contained a demand for a graduated, or progressive, income tax. Two years later, Congress passed the Wilson-Gorman Tariff Act, which, among other things, set up an income tax

What: Law and economics
When: February 25, 1913
Where: Washington, D.C.
Who:
JOSEPH WELDON BAILEY (1863-1929), Senator from Texas from 1901 to 1913
ALBERT CUMMINS (1850-1926), Senator from Iowa from 1908 to 1926
NELSON ALDRICH (1841-1915), Senator from Rhode Island from 1881 to 1911
WILLIAM HOWARD TAFT (1857-1930) President of the United States from 1909 to 1913

of 2 percent on all incomes over four thousand dollars. In 1895, however, the Supreme Court declared the income tax unconstitutional in *Pollock* v. *Farmers' Loan and Trust*, since the Constitution prohibited direct taxation.

Those who favored the income tax did not agree with the Supreme Court's interpretation of the Constitution, and they continued to fight for the tax. Wealth was being concentrated more and more in the hands of a few, and many Americans considered this a direct threat to democracy. The income tax seemed a way of reversing that trend, of redistributing some wealth to those who had less.

One of the leaders of the struggle for an income tax was Senator Joseph W. Bailey, a Democrat from Texas. In April, 1909, Bailey proposed an

103

VOL. XXXVII. No. 949. PUCK BUILDING, New York, May 15th, 1895. PRICE 10 CENTS.
Copyright, 1895, by Keppler & Schwarzmann.

Puck

"What fools these Mortals be."

Entered at N. Y. P. O. as Second-class Mail Matter.

WITHOUT A FRIEND.

income-tax amendment to the Payne-Aldrich Tariff Bill, which Congress was considering at that time. Bailey suggested a 3 percent tax on all incomes over five thousand dollars. His idea was soon replaced, however, with a more radical proposal by Albert Cummins, Senator from Iowa: a graduated income tax ranging from 2 percent on incomes over five thousand dollars to 6 percent on incomes over $100,000.

The Amendment

Conservative Democrats and Republicans, led by Senator Nelson Aldrich of Rhode Island, did not think that taxes should be used to try to redistribute wealth. When they realized that the income-tax amendment to the tariff bill might have enough votes to pass, Senator Aldrich and President William Howard Taft suggested that a constitutional amendment should be passed to make sure that the income tax was legal.

Although those who favored the income tax feared that the amendment was the conservatives' attempt at defeating or at least delaying any income tax, they finally agreed to the idea of a constitutional amendment. In July, 1909, the amendment was put before the states.

The road to ratification was not easy. Through-out 1910 and 1911, Republican and Democratic conservatives attacked the amendment, saying that it would lead the United States down the path to socialism. Yet in the state governments the forces of Progressivism were strong, and in the end, only five states did not ratify the amendment. On February 25, 1913, Secretary of State Philander C. Knox certified that the Sixteenth Amendment was officially part of the Constitution.

Consequences

Soon after the ratification of the Sixteenth Amendment, Congress passed the first income-tax law as part of the Underwood-Simmons Tariff Act. Although by modern standards the rate of taxation was low, the bill set an important precedent by making the income tax progressive. The Sixteenth Amendment had made no mention of graduated rates of taxation, but from that time forward they were accepted as a fair way of structuring the income tax. In this way, more of the tax burden was shifted to those who were best able to pay.

The income tax did reverse the trend toward concentration of wealth. After 1913, the poorer classes carried a smaller share of taxation in the United States.

A cartoon appearing in the 1895 issue of *Puck* depicts the Supreme Court's determination, in that year, that income tax was unconstitutional. (*Library of Congress*)

FORD DEVELOPS THE ASSEMBLY LINE

In his manufacturing plants in Detroit, Michigan, Henry Ford and a team of engineers refined the concept of the assembly line to allow for a much faster production of automobiles.

What: Economics
When: March 1, 1913-January 5, 1914
Where: Detroit, Michigan
Who:
HENRY FORD (1863-1947), the head of the Ford Motor Company
CHARLES SORENSEN (1882-1968), a technician who contributed to the moving assembly line
WILLIAM C. KLANN (dates unknown), a technician who adapted the idea to the assembly of motors
CARL EMDE (dates unknown), a German technician who built machinery for Ford
JAMES COUZENS (1872-1936), Ford's business manager

New Methods

Mass production and the assembly line are often thought of in connection with Henry Ford, but these methods were not actually his original ideas. The three basic ideas of mass production—standardization, simplification, and interchangeability—date back to the eighteenth century. Before 1913, there were a number of companies that produced such things as telephone sets, bicycles, typewriters, and cash registers in large quantities. Ford himself had an assembly-line system in his original plant; it produced a car every thirteen hours.

After the opening of the Ford Motor Company in 1903, Ford decided that he would produce only one type of automobile, the Model T. Rival companies, which were manufacturing a number of different models, believed this decision would doom Ford's business to failure. Ford's idea was to keep his car's design standard and invest most of his money, time, and effort on the equipment and machinery to produce it. He wanted to "build a motor car for the great multitude"—for average middle-class Americans—and this goal could be achieved only if he produced large numbers of cars and was able to keep their prices low.

Early in 1907, the plant slowed down as it switched over to the production of Model T's only. This plant, in the Piquette area, had within it a number of assembly-line techniques: Work was brought to the workers, and the men, machines, and materials were placed in a logical arrangement that followed the order in which the cars were assembled. About twelve thousand cars were produced in this plant in 1909.

In the following year, Ford moved into a plant in the Highland Park area and greatly expanded his factory. There, between 1912 and 1913, the continuous assembly line was developed. The new techniques were aimed at increasing "power, accuracy, economy, system, continuity, speed, repetition." Ford's assistants in the design of this project included Carl Emde, who created the necessary machinery; William C. Klann, who worked with the system to make it useful for the assembly of motors; and Charles Sorensen, who added the idea of the continuous conveyor belt and who completed the assembly line.

Although there is no detailed record of the steps in the designing and building of the contin-

Ford Motor Company's Highland Park assembly line, c. 1913. (*Library of Congress*)

uous assembly line, it is known that it was in operation by March 1, 1913. The main assembly line had forty-five operations, and it quickly increased the speed of production. A motor that had previously taken one person 600 minutes to assemble could now be put together in 226 minutes. A chassis that had taken one person 12 hours and 28 minutes to complete could now be finished in 1 hour and 33 minutes. The plant that had produced 78,440 automobiles in 1911-1912 was by 1916-1917 producing 730,041 automobiles — or 2,000 each day.

The Human Factor

The Ford Motor Company grew very rapidly and was on its way to becoming the largest manufacturer of cars in the United States. Yet its methods began to be criticized. The use of ma-

chines and the division of each job into many small, repetitive tasks meant that most factory work required very little real skill. (The exceptions were the jobs of a few top engineers who designed the product and process.)

Sociologists and social reformers began to protest the dreary monotony of the endless repetition of work. As if to confirm their complaints, workers began to leave Ford at an alarming rate.

Beginning in 1913, the Ford Motor Company introduced "the most advanced labor policies yet known in large-scale American industry." Safety measures were improved and extended, the workday was reduced to eight hours, and the factory was converted to run on three shifts instead of two. Aptitude tests, sick-leave allowances, an English-language school for immigrants, a technical school, better medical care for the injured,

and an improved factory environment were all soon introduced. The company even made special efforts to hire persons with disabilities and former convicts.

The most remarkable new policy of all, however, was the five-dollar minimum wage. This policy was announced by Henry Ford and his company's business manager, James Couzens, on January 5, 1914. Various reasons have been suggested to explain this decision: to get the pick of Detroit mechanics; to keep workers for a longer time and reduce turnover; to respond to the threat of unionization by the Industrial Workers of the World; and to motivate employees to be agreeable to a new speedup of work at the plant.

The reason Ford himself gave was "profit sharing and efficiency engineering." The company was enjoying a very large net income and wanted to share some of it with the workers. Furthermore, a higher wage would mean more loyal, better disciplined, and more efficient and productive workers.

To qualify for the five-dollar minimum wage, each employee had to meet certain standards: to be a person of good personal habits with a decent home and, if under twenty-two years of age, to prove himself to be "sober, saving, steady, industrious." To find out which employees met these standards, and to help those who did not, the company created a "Sociological Department."

Consequences

There is no question that assembly lines have greatly increased the efficiency of manufacturing and packaging. Yet criticism of continuous assembly lines has continued throughout the twentieth century. Assembly-line work is seen as numbing to the mind, and increasingly it has been recognized that continuously repetitive movements can be physically harmful.

In the second half of the twentieth century, there has been experimentation with other styles of manufacturing. Some research indicates that workers' satisfaction with their work increases greatly when their job is set up so that they can see a product develop from beginning to end. Another option has been to design machines that can take over tiresomely repetitive tasks. Yet regardless of whether modern factories use a version of Ford's continuous assembly line, it is clear that his values of speed and efficiency continue to influence the way manufacturing is carried out.

CONGRESS PASSES THE FEDERAL RESERVE ACT

The Federal Reserve Act established a system designed to promote a stable dollar and orderly growth in the economy of the United States.

Need for Banking Reform

By the beginning of the twentieth century the American economy was the most powerful in the world, yet the country's banking system was old-fashioned and inadequate. The United States had two types of commercial banks: those chartered by the states and those having national charters from the federal government. Under the National Bank acts of 1863 and 1864, national banks were required to buy government securities and to be regulated by the federal government, but they could issue national bank notes, a fairly stable paper currency.

The nation's banking system, made up of state and national banks, had many problems. Banking laws varied from one state to the next, and some states were lax in regulating banking activity. State bank charters could be obtained so easily that there were many banks that were mismanaged and lost the depositors' money. National banks tended to be more stable than state banks, but at critical moments national banks often found it difficult to get needed cash.

The major problems all banks faced was that the currency supply was "inelastic" — that is, neither banks nor the government had the power to expand or contract the money supply to meet the seasonal needs of industry and farming, or to prevent financial panics.

In the late nineteenth century, various reform measures were proposed to meet these needs. Among the most popular were the Greenback movement of the 1870's and the Populists' proposal for a Subtreasury Plan and for the free and unlimited coinage of silver in the 1890's. Many

What: Economics
When: December, 1913
Where: Washington, D.C.
Who:
NELSON ALDRICH (1841-1915),
    Republican Senator from Rhode
    Island from 1881 to 1911
WILLIAM JENNINGS BRYAN (1860-1925),
    a Democratic leader from Nebraska
· CARTER GLASS (1858-1946), a
    conservative Democratic
    Congressman from Virginia from
    1902 to 1919
WILLIAM GIBBS MCADOO (1863-1941),
    Secretary of the Treasury from 1913
    to 1918
ROBERT LATHAM OWEN (1856-1947),
    Democratic Senator from Oklahoma
HENRY PARKER WILLIS (1874-1937), a
    bank expert
WOODROW WILSON (1856-1924),
    President of the United States from
    1913 to 1921

who were more conservative believed it would be helpful to establish a central bank — rather like the Bank of England — to hold government deposits and central banking reserves and to have full responsibility for the issuing of paper money.

The financial panic of 1907 clearly showed the weakness of the banking system. Throughout the country, depositors hurried to their banks to withdraw their savings; even banks that had been well managed were unable to meet the flood of demands. This crisis led to more calls for banking reform.

The Act Is Passed

In 1908, Congress created the National Monetary Commission, made up of members of Congress, to make a plan for revision of the banking system. Headed by Senator Nelson Aldrich, the commission drew up the so-called Aldrich Plan. It called for a voluntary system headed by a central bank, the National Reserve Association. With its branch banks, the National Reserve would issue currency, hold the deposits of the federal government, and furnish reserve credit to member banks.

Some large banks supported the Aldrich Plan, but by the time it was submitted to Congress in 1912 it faced strong opposition. Many Progres-

sives believed that the plan would allow large financial institutions even more control over the nation's money. They were relieved when Woodrow Wilson was elected president in 1912.

Although the Democrats controlled the new Congress, they were divided on the issue of banking. On one side were the Southern and Western radicals who followed William Jennings Bryan of Nebraska. On the other were conservatives headed by Congressman Carter Glass of Virginia, chairman of the House Banking Committee. Bryan, who was joined by William McAdoo, soon to be Secretary of the Treasury, and Senator Robert L. Owen of Oklahoma, insisted that any new banking system be under the government's full control, and that the government control and guarantee the currency supply. Glass and his followers opposed any plan for a central bank;

they wanted to see a loose, disconnected system of regional reserve banks.

In the weeks before Wilson was inaugurated, he received help from Glass and banking expert H. Parker Willis to draft a new banking law. They proposed a privately controlled system of regional reserve banks under a general board that would coordinate and supervise their activities. This was actually a decentralized version of the Aldrich Plan. Glass gave in to certain wishes of Bryan's faction and added to the bill a federal guarantee of the notes issued by the new system.

The plan was put before Congress as the Federal Reserve Bill (also called the Glass-Owen Bill). More changes were made in committee, and the measure was finally passed in December, 1913.

The Federal Reserve Act was intended to establish no more than twelve Federal Reserve banks, to allow for an elastic currency, and to make the supervision of banking in the United States more effective. The twelve "bankers' banks" do not accept deposits from individuals or loan money to them. They are controlled by a board of governors (originally with five members, later seven) appointed by the President of the United States for ten-year terms. The board works with the Secretary of the Treasury and the Comptroller of the Currency to supervise the system.

All national banks are required to belong to the system, but state banks and trust companies can also join if they meet certain requirements. Member banks elect six of the nine directors of the district Federal Reserve banks. Although the system is a corporation owned by the member commercial banks, the Federal Reserve is in fact a public agency. It is directly responsible to Congress, some of its officials are appointed by the president, and it has traditionally put the public interest before private profit.

Consequences

The Federal Reserve Act created a system that did solve some banking problems in the United States. It allowed for a more elastic currency and system of making loans. Yet it has not been able to eliminate financial crises. There was wild inflation in the United States during World War I, while in 1921, there was a brief but severe financial depression. Throughout the 1920's, many banks failed. The Federal Reserve banks allowed too much money to be invested in risky ventures during that period, and in this way they contributed to the stock-market crash of 1929. In the 1920's, the Federal Reserve Bank of New York dominated the system, and as Bryan's followers had feared, New York-based banks and corporations increased their hold on the country's supply of credit.

The nation's worst economic crisis and the "holiday" that closed all the banks of the country took place in the 1930's. Only then were measures taken to insure depositors' money against loss and to regulate the banking system more strictly. In spite of these changes, the Federal Reserve System exists today in the same basic form as when it was created in 1913.

Carter Glass, one of the bill's authors. (*AP/Wide World Photos*)

The Assassination of Archduke Ferdinand Begins World War I

After the heir apparent to the throne of Austria-Hungary was killed by a Serbian nationalist, aggression and mistrust spread quickly beyond Austria and Serbia, so that all Europe became engulfed in war.

What: Military conflict
When: June 28, 1914
Where: Europe
Who:
ARCHDUKE FRANCIS FERDINAND (1863-1914), heir apparent of Austria-Hungary
COUNT LEOPOLD VON BERCHTOLD (1863-1942), Foreign Minister of Austria-Hungary from 1912 to 1915
SERGEI DMITRIEVICH SAZONOV (1861-1927), Russian Minister of Foreign Affairs from 1910 to 1916
SIR EDWARD GREY (1862-1933), Foreign Secretary of Great Britain from 1905 to 1916
THEOBALD VON BETHMANN-HOLLWEG (1856-1921), Chancellor of the German Empire from 1909 to 1917

Assassination and Ultimatum

On June 28, 1914, Gavrilo Princip, a Bosnian member of a Serbian terrorist organization, shot and killed Archduke Francis Ferdinand, heir apparent to the throne of Austria-Hungary, and his wife. The assassination took place in Sarajevo, the capital of Bosnia-Hercegovina, which had been annexed by Austria-Hungary but whose population was mostly Serbian.

Austrian leaders quickly decided to use the occasion to force a diplomatic confrontation with Serbia. For a long time, Serbians had called fellow Slavs within the Austrian Empire to join them in creating a great Slavic nation, and Austria now suspected the Serbian government of having supported the plot to assassinate Francis Ferdinand.

With the support of Germany, Austria wrote an ultimatum to present to the Serbian government. The ultimatum's demands were quite severe, and Serbia was given only two days to comply. Yet on July 25, Serbia agreed to nearly all the Austrians' demands.

Austria-Hungary and its main ally, Germany, apparently thought that Serbia's ally Russia would avoid becoming involved in the conflict. Though Russia had a long-standing interest in Serbia and the other Balkan States, leaders of Austria and Germany decided that Russia would have too much to lose by joining the dispute. Even if Russia and its ally France intervened, they thought, the other member of the Triple Entente, Great Britain, would remain neutral.

So it was that Austria-Hungary, declaring that Serbia had not met all of its demands, broke off all diplomatic relations with Serbia and prepared for war. The formal declaration of war came on July 28, 1914.

War Breaks Out

The Austrians had not understood the Russians' position. Russia had been defeated in two important wars—the Crimean War of 1853-1856 and the Russo-Japanese War of 1904-1905—and

The emperor (left) and the archduke. (*National Archives*)

had suffered a diplomatic embarrassment in the Balkans in 1909. Its leaders wanted to restore their country to a place of world leadership and respect, and they did not want to be humiliated again.

For these reasons, Russia responded to Austria-Hungary with heat. On July 28, the same day that Austria declared war on Serbia, Czar Nicholas II and his council of ministers ordered the Russian army to begin mobilizing — gearing up for the possibility of war. Two days later, Nicholas announced an all-out mobilization of Russia's troops.

Within Russia, there was widespread support for the war effort. Though the Bolsheviks opposed war, other parties, both conservative and liberal, agreed that Russia should be willing to fight if necessary.

Great Britain and Germany had both made efforts to end the crisis through some kind of international conference, but their attempts led nowhere. Germany's plan of defense was based on its ability to mobilize quickly and to act more swiftly than its enemies. Now German officials believed their country to be in serious danger from Russia. Having sent a "war warning" to Russia, Germany began mobilizing on August 1. France started mobilizing its army the same day.

Germany declared war on Russia on August 1, and two days later it declared war on France. Russia was deep in its own preparations for war. On August 4, Germany began an invasion of Belgium. In response, that same day Great Britain joined the fray. World War I had begun.

Consequences

The Great War, as it has come to be called, was the product of tensions that had been building throughout Europe for many years. One key element in these tensions was the drive to build empires — to extend national influence into weaker countries, not only in Africa, Asia, and South America but also in the Balkan States of southeastern Europe.

World War I was a long, bloody, expensive conflict. One of its effects was the breaking up of the European empires. Throughout the twentieth century, colony after colony gained independence, and the European powers eventually retreated, for the most part, from ambitions of vast political empires.

FRANCE AND GERMANY CLASH IN THE FIRST BATTLE OF THE MARNE

> *With a French and British victory in a battle in the Marne Valley, German attempts to gain control of the European continent were frustrated.*

Strategies

Before the outbreak of World War I, General Alfred von Schlieffen, Chief of Staff of the German Army from 1891 to 1906, developed a plan to be followed in case of war with France and Russia. He knew that the vast size of Russia and its lack of a good railroad system meant that the Russian reserve divisions and the Siberian armies could not be made ready for war on the German frontier with less than two months' preparation time. France, on the other hand, was a much smaller country and had a dense network of railroads; it could bring up all of its troops against Germany in three weeks.

In light of these realities, Schlieffen planned that seven of the eight German armies would be sent up against the French at first. His proposal was to send two strong armies through Belgium toward the west and then wheel them southward, with the German First Army, on the right of the advance, passing west of Paris. The French armies would be trapped in a pocket southeast of Paris, and they would be forced to surrender. German forces could then be sent to the Eastern Front to fight the Russians, who were expected to have gotten as far as East Prussia by then, but no farther than the Vistula River in Poland. If this plan were followed, Schlieffen estimated that the war would be over in about four months.

General Helmuth von Moltke succeeded General Schlieffen as Chief of Staff of the German Army in 1906. Fearful that the French might invade German Alsace while the right wing of

What: Military conflict
When: September 6-9, 1914
Where: The Marne Valley, east of Paris
Who:
GENERAL ALFRED VON SCHLIEFFEN (1833-1913), Chief of Staff of the German Army from 1891 to 1906
GENERAL HELMUTH VON MOLTKE (1848-1916), Chief of Staff of the German Army from 1906 to 1914
GENERAL ALEXANDER VON KLUCK (1846-1934), Commander of the First Army of Germany
GENERAL KARL VON BÜLOW (1846-1921), Commander of the Second Army of Germany
GENERAL JOSEPH-JACQUES-CÉSAIRE JOFFRE (1852-1931), Commander in Chief of the French Armies from 1914 to 1916
GENERAL JOSEPH-SIMON GALLIENI (1849-1916), Military Governor of Paris from 1914 to 1915
GENERAL LOUIS-FÉLIX-MARIE-FRANÇOIS FRANCHET D'ESPEREY (1856-1942), Commander of the Fifth Army of France
FIELD MARSHAL SIR JOHN DENTON FRENCH (1852-1925), Commander in Chief of the British Expeditionary Force

the German forces was still advancing, Moltke changed Schlieffen's plan somewhat to strengthen the army's left flank with new divisions. These new divisions were formed before 1913.

Battle in the Marne

With the outbreak of World War I in 1914, Moltke's version of Schlieffen's plan was put into action. The German First and Second armies, with thirty-two of the seventy-eight German infantry divisions in the West, began to move through Belgium. Meanwhile, the French began to fight the advancing Germans directly. Between August 20 and 24, 1914, a series of small but bloody battles took place along the border between France and Belgium.

Although the Germans were attacking, they were often in the defensive position, having to protect themselves against French onslaughts. Yet the German artillery and machine guns did turn back the French attacks. On August 25, General Joseph-Jacques-Césaire Joffre, Commander in Chief of the French Armies, was forced to order a general retreat of all the French armies. German troops followed close behind.

At the same time, France's allies were mobilizing and sending troops. The British Expeditionary Force, commanded by Field Marshal Sir John Denton French, entered the fight on August 23. Three days later, Joffre ordered the formation of a new French Sixth Army in Paris, under the orders of the capital's military governor, General Joseph-Simon Gallieni.

Moltke was still determined to get past the French Fifth Army at the Franco-Belgian border. On August 30, he decided not to follow Schlieffen's plan of an advance to the west of Paris. Instead, he directed the German First Army to advance east of Paris, one day's march behind the German Second Army.

The proud commander of the German First Army, General Alexander von Kluck, disobeyed the order and continued to move his army forward in line with the German Second Army, com-

manded by General Karl von Bülow, on his left. Kluck did move one army corps from his left to his right as a flanking guard against forces that might come from Paris, but this maneuver opened a small gap between his forces and Bülow's.

On September 3, aware that Kluck's and Bülow's forces were slightly separated, Gallieni suggested attacking Kluck's army. Joffre responded on September 4, by ordering an "about-face" of the Allied armies, and a general offensive against the Germans began on September 6.

When Gallieni's troops came up to Kluck's flanking guard, Kluck transferred more men from his left to his right in order to avoid being overcome from the rear. As a result, the gap between his army and Bülow's widened to about twenty miles. If their armies had had the extra troops that Moltke had assigned to the left flank at the beginning of the war, there might have been no gap, and the Battle of the Marne might have turned out differently.

On September 6, the French Fifth Army, under the command of General Louis-Félix-Marie-François Franchet d'Esperey, and the British Expeditionary Force, sent forward by Field Marshal French, moved slowly into the gap to threaten the flanks of the German First and Second armies. There was little serious fighting. The Germans were alarmed and fell back to regroup and prepare a new move to try to outflank the French. Their retreat ended the First Battle of the Marne.

Consequences

The German plan to overwhelm France quickly and then crush Russia with Austria-Hungary's help was frustrated by the French victory at Marne. The Germans would now have to face a long conflict on the Western Front, with Allied troops established in position. Joffre's decision to stop the withdrawal of the French armies and to counterattack stopped the German invasion, saved the French from defeat, and kept the Germans from winning quick control over Europe.

General Joffre, hero of the Marne (*AP/Wide World Photos*)

Submarine Warfare Begins

With the Germans' use of submarines to attack British ships in World War I, a new era of war at sea was launched.

What: Military conflict and technological advance
When: September 22, 1914
Where: The southern North Sea
Who:
Vice Admiral Prince Louis Alexander of Battenberg (1854-1921), First Sea Lord of the British Admiralty from 1912 to 1914
Admiral Henry H. Campbell (1865-1933), Commander of the British Seventh Cruiser Squadron
Lieutenant Otto Weddigen (1882-1915), Captain of the German submarine *U-9*

The First Attacks

At the beginning of World War I, the First Sea Lord of the British Admiralty, Vice Admiral Prince Louis Alexander of Battenberg, set up patrols in the southern North Sea to protect the eastern entrance of the English Channel against raids by German destroyers and minelayers. The force that was assigned to this task included two flotillas of destroyers and a squadron of five old armored cruisers. Copies of the orders given at the time show that British naval officers were not taking seriously the possibility of an attack from German submarines.

On September 5, 1941, the British light cruiser H.M.S. *Pathfinder* was sunk by the German submarine *U-21* off the Firth of Forth. On September 13, the British submarine *E-9* was able to destroy the German light cruiser *Hela* off Heligoland. These events should have made it clear that the submarine was making its appearance in war and would have to be seen as a serious danger to surface ships. Yet the First Sea Lord did nothing to prepare the southern patrol for further submarine attacks.

On September 22, three ships of the British Seventh Cruiser Squadron, H.M.S. *Aboukir*, *Cressy*, and *Hogue*, were patrolling west of the Dutch coast. The squadron commander, Admiral Henry H. Campbell, was on his flagship, which was refueling in port. When bad weather drove the escorting destroyers into port, the three cruisers were left unprotected. Following the admiral's orders, they were steaming on a straight course at less than ten knots per hour.

Soon after sunrise, they were sighted by Lieutenant Otto Weddigen, Captain of the German submarine *U-9*. At 6:30 A.M. he hit the *Aboukir* with a single, well-directed torpedo. The cruiser quickly sloped dangerously to one side.

The captain of the *Aboukir*, Captain John E. Drummond, believed that he had hit a mine, and, being the senior officer, he ordered the other two British cruisers to come close to his ship. The *Hogue* neared the sinking ship, came to a stop, and launched its boats to rescue the crew of the *Aboukir*. *U-9* then took aim at the *Hogue*, which was sitting still, and fired at close range. Two torpedoes hit their mark.

The *Aboukir*, meanwhile, capsized and sank. Ten minutes later the *Hogue* sank as well, and its survivors joined those from the *Aboukir* in the sea. Unwilling to abandon the struggling men,

The engine room of an oil-burning German submarine. (*National Archives*)

Captain R. W. Johnson of the *Cressy* brought his vessel to a dead stop and thus provided another helpless target for the *U-9*.

Weddigen did not miss the opportunity. He reloaded his torpedo tubes and fired three missiles at the *Cressy*. Two torpedoes exploded against it, ripping out its side. The cruiser rolled over on its beam-ends, hung there while it filled, and then sank in fifteen minutes.

In just over an hour, Weddigen had sunk three 12,000-ton armored cruisers with his small 493-ton submarine, manned by twenty-nine men. The British loss of life was very heavy; fourteen hundred men out of the twenty-two hundred in the three ships' crews were either killed by the torpedoes or drowned.

The Attacks Spread

Soon after this disaster, German submarines began to attack merchant vessels, and they proved to be very effective destroyers of naval commerce. On October 20, 1914, *U-17* sank the British *Glitra*; this was the first of more than thirteen thousand merchant ships, thirty-six million tons in all, to be sunk by submarines of all navies in World Wars I and II.

In 1917, the Germans began a campaign of unrestricted submarine warfare. "Unrestricted" meant that the U-boats did not follow the rules of international law, which said that warship crews must search merchant ships suspected of carrying contraband before destroying them. According to international law, merchant ships were not to be

sunk at all if the crew could not first be put in a safe place.

Through unrestricted torpedo attacks and minelaying in the first four months of 1917, German submarines sank 1,147 ships, totaling 2,224,000 tons. As a result, Great Britain faced the possibility of starvation and defeat. The British responded by collecting their merchant ships into convoys, so that they could be directly protected by an escort of warships.

Consequences

The Germans' attack against commercial shipping was considered cowardly and uncivilized by the standards of those days. This was the development that brought the United States into the war against Germany. Clearly, submarine warfare was one of Germany's most important strategies throughout World War I.

In World War II, the British and their allies used the convoy system to protect merchant ships from the beginning. The Germans retaliated by grouping their U-boats into packs. Packs of five or ten submarines and the convoy escorts fought one another fiercely during the grim Battle of the Atlantic. In 1942 alone, German submarines sank 1,054 ships totaling 5,764,000 tons — a very serious set of losses for the Allies. In the Mediterranean, British submarines were successful in sinking a quarter of the entire Italian merchant marine. In this way the British helped to cut off the Italian and German armies in Libya from their sources of food, fuel, and ammunition.

SPAIN DECLARES NEUTRALITY IN WORLD WAR I

Though Spain's leaders decided to keep the country out of World War I because of internal divisions, the war served to make the divisions more serious, so that Spain's constitutional government finally fell apart.

The Necessary Neutrality

When World War I broke out in August, 1914, Spain was a deeply divided nation. Some powerful groups supported the Allies, while other equally powerful ones supported the Central Powers. All agreed, however, that Spain would be better off by remaining neutral in the conflict. There was a general sense that Spain's internal problems were more important at the time than foreign issues.

After Conservative Prime Minister Eduardo Dato Iradier declared the neutrality of Spain, his declaration was confirmed by the Cortes (the Spanish parliament), when it met on October 30, 1914.

For some time, Spain's opposing parties had taken turns governing the country for agreed-upon periods of time. This system had broken down, however, by 1914. Demands for reform were fought bitterly in the Cortes and aroused violence across the country. The republicans, led by Radical Republican Alejandro Lerroux García, had been growing into a sizable force, and so had the Socialists and the anarchists. Even the Conservatives had been preaching the cause of reform—especially Antonio Maura y Montaner. He demanded that the government begin "reform from above" so that the people would not rebel and start a revolution.

Weathering the War

At first, World War I had a positive effect on Spain. Trade increased enormously, as orders poured in from nations involved in fighting. In-

What: International relations
When: October 30, 1914
Where: Madrid
Who:
EDUARDO DATO IRADIER (1856-1921), Conservative Prime Minister of Spain from 1913 to 1915 and in 1917
ALEJANDRO LERROUX GARCÍA (1864-1949), a Radical Republican leader
ANTONIO MAURA Y MONTANER (1853-1925), a Conservative leader, and Prime Minister in 1918 and 1919
ÁLVARO DE FIGUEROA Y DE TORRES, CONDE DE ROMANONES (1863-1950), Liberal Prime Minister in 1915
FRANCISCO CAMBÓ (dates unknown), leader of the Catalan Lliga
MANUEL GARCÍA PRIETO, MARQUÉS DE ALHUEMAS (dates unknown), Liberal Prime Minister from 1917 to 1918

vestment funds from abroad increased as well. Spain suddenly found itself exporting more goods than it imported. An industrial boom led factories to operate overtime, and there was no unemployment in industrial areas.

Yet the boom also brought inflation. Wages kept up with prices in only a few industries, so that most of the Spanish people found that their money covered fewer of their expenses. Soon the working classes threatened to strike unless the government took action to stop rising prices.

The Conservative government of Dato Iradier could not control this unrest, and late in 1915 it was replaced by the Liberal government of Conde de Romanones. Romanones faced two big problems. First, the younger army officers had responded to inflation by organizing their own association, similar to a union, to help them get higher pay and to demand that political promotions within the army come to an end. Most working-class organizations, along with the country's intellectuals, sympathized with the goals of this group, seeing it as a reforming trade-union movement within the army. The Catalans were also supportive.

The people of Catalonia, in response to the Industrial Revolution and a cultural renaissance in the late nineteenth century, had begun a strong movement for their region's independence. They complained that the Madrid government stood in the way of their well-being and that their taxes were being used to support the rest of Spain. Catalan leaders in business and industry formed the Lliga, an organization to protest Madrid's policies and to demand that Catalonia be given greater control over its own affairs.

The coming of World War I made the Catalan problem more intense. Because Barcelona, the principal city in Catalonia, was the nation's largest center of industry and trade, inflation and other economic problems became worst there.

The Lliga, led by Francisco Cambó, demanded that Barcelona be made a free port. Romanones refused, and his government fell in 1915.

Romanones' successor was Manuel García Prieto, Marqués de Alhuemas, another Liberal. He also failed to solve the nation's problems, and the

Conservative Dato Iradier was returned to leadership in 1917.

By then, the crisis in Spain had grown out of hand. The Catalans, the young army officers, the Socialists, Lerroux, and Maura all joined in demanding that a special Cortes be gathered to draft a new constitution for the country. Dato Iradier refused and, saying that the situation demanded emergency measures, took away the freedoms promised by the Spanish constitutions.

The response was a general strike, and the army was called to put it to an end. With this act, parliamentary government in Spain ended; the army was now the ruling force in the country. The army took charge completely in 1923.

Consequences

Spain was in no condition to send an army into World War I, and its leaders were only displaying common sense when they decided to declare neutrality. Yet the war still affected the country deeply. With prices rising faster than incomes, the people of Spain found it more and more difficult to meet their daily expenses.

As their discontent increased, they continued to divide into hostile factions. All the groups became less and less willing to accept the inadequate solutions their government offered. The end result was the collapse of parliamentary government in Spain.

Spanish officers visiting Allied forces in France. (*National Archives*)

JAPAN PRESENTS CHINA WITH THE TWENTY-ONE DEMANDS

With a list of demands for increased political, military, and economic rights, Japan tried to become the controlling foreign power in China.

What: International relations
When: January 18, 1915
Where: Japan and China
Who:

YÜAN SHIH-K'AI (1859-1916), President of China from 1912 to 1916

BARON TAKAAKIRA KATO (1859-1926), Foreign Minister of Japan from 1914 to 1915

ARIGA NAGAO (1860-1921), Japanese adviser to Yüan Shih-k'ai

WOODROW WILSON (1856-1924), President of the United States from 1913 to 1921

PAUL SAMUEL REINSCH (1869-1923), United States Ambassador to China from 1913 to 1919

SIR EDWARD GREY (1862-1933), Foreign Secretary of Great Britain from 1905 to 1916

JOHN NEWELL JORDAN (1852-1925), British Minister to China from 1906 to 1920

Reaching for Power

The island nation of Japan borrowed many of its traditions from China, and there have always been similarities of culture between the two countries. The Buddhist religion first came to Japan from China, and the Japanese system of writing is based on that of China.

In the early twentieth century, however, the international status of the two countries was quite different. Under the Manchu emperors, China had remained wrapped up in the traditions of the past, while greedy Western states took more and more special privileges for their business interests within the country. China's Republican Revolution of 1911 did not stop the country's decline.

Japan, on the other hand, had successfully reformed its economy, army, and school system, though it had kept the traditional imperial form of government. In the Sino-Japanese War of 1895, Japan was strong enough to defeat the much larger China on the field of battle. As a result, Japan annexed the island of Taiwan and gained great influence over the kingdom of Korea. Japan also joined the soldiers of the Western nations to defeat the Chinese who rose up against foreign domination in the Boxer Rebellion of 1900. Clearly, Japan was moving toward building its own empire.

In August, 1914, Takaakira Kato, who had become Foreign Minister of Japan earlier that year, led his country into World War I on the side of Great Britain, which had been Japan's ally since 1902. Japanese forces soon took over the land Germany had been leasing in the Chinese province of Shantung.

Kato believed in government by political parties, and he wanted to get rid of the traditional power of the elder statesmen, or genro, in Japanese politics. Now he thought he saw an opportunity. If he could gain new power for Japan within China, perhaps he could win the political struggle at home. With the European powers tied up in World War I, China would be quite helpless and Japan could gain valuable advantages.

So it was that on January 18, 1915, Hioki Eki,

President Wilson expressed objections to the Twenty-one Demands on the part of the United States. (*AP/Wide World Photos*)

Japanese Minister to China, presented to Chinese President Yüan Shih-k'ai a series of proposals that came to be known as the Twenty-one Demands. These demands were divided into five groups. In groups one through four, Japan demanded that China's government approve Japan's recent gains in Shantung and its privileges in overseeing certain territories, trade, and railroads in Manchuria. China was also asked to promise never to let any other power lease or gain control over any harbor, bay, or island along its coast.

It was the group five demands, however, that were most serious. China was to consult with Japan before allowing any foreign investments in the Fukien Province. Japan also demanded new rights over railroads in the Yangtze River Valley and said that China must buy at least half of its arms from Japan. What is more, the Chinese government would be required to hire Japanese men as political, financial, and military advisers, and to share with Japan the control of the police forces in certain parts of China. If China had agreed to all these terms, it would have become a protectorate of Japan.

Responding to the Demands

President Yüan knew that because of his country's military weakness, it could not resist Japan on its own. He would have to make sure other nations became involved. So when negotiations

began, he stalled for time, dragging the talks out as long as possible. The talks were supposed to be secret, but Yüan made sure that United States Ambassador Paul Samuel Reinsch and British Ambassador John Newell Jordan found out what was going on.

At first, this strategy seemed to be working. Reinsch sent numerous telegrams to U.S. President Woodrow Wilson, urging him to protect China. Wilson was quite disturbed by Japan's bullying of China, for the American policy had been to keep any single power from dominating that vast country. On March 13, 1915, the U.S. government sent a note to Japan, expressing its objections to various parts of the Twenty-one Demands.

When British Foreign Secretary Sir Edward Grey learned from Jordan about Japan's demands, he, too, became alarmed. He wanted to keep Japan as an ally of Great Britain, yet he did not want Japan to elbow Great Britain out of its rights in China. So on May 3, 1915, the British government followed the United States' lead and sent a note to Japan, objecting to the Twenty-one Demands.

Yüan, meanwhile, sent Ariga Nagao, a Japanese adviser who was loyal to China, to the Japanese capital of Tokyo. There Ariga warned various Japanese politicians that Kato's policy might lead Great Britain to abandon Japan as an ally. Many of the Japanese genro, who had great influence over Japan's cabinet, were persuaded by his arguments.

On May 4, 1915, just after Japan had received Great Britain's warning, the Japanese cabinet held an emergency meeting. Its decision was to alter Kato's China policy. Two days later, Japan would insist that China meet certain of its demands, but none of the demands of group five would be included. China was given until May 9, to accept the first four groups of the original Twenty-one Demands. If it refused, Japan would declare war.

British Ambassador Jordan urged Yüan to accept this reduced set of demands as soon as possible. The Americans had become preoccupied by their deteriorating relations with Germany, so that they had lost interest in backing China. Yüan felt compelled to sign a treaty with Japan, granting all the first four groups of the Twenty-one Demands. He did so on May 25, 1915.

Consequences

Within Japan, many nationalists were not satisfied with the terms of the treaty. Many of them blamed Great Britain for limiting Japan's gains. As a result, in August, 1915, Kato resigned from the Foreign Ministry; he would never hold office again.

Many Chinese nationalists were similarly upset. They saw the treaty as a national humiliation, and a new wave of anger against foreigners — Japanese and Westerners alike — swept across the country. When the 1919 Treaty of Versailles confirmed Japan's gains in the province of Shantung, the Chinese became even more enraged.

The United States continued to be concerned about Japanese expansion in China. On May 11, 1915, U.S. Secretary of State William Jennings Bryan publicly warned Japan that the United States would not recognize any agreement that damaged China as a sovereign state. Great Britain eventually followed suit: In 1923, wishing to please the United States, it ended its alliance with Japan. The end result of the break between Japan and its former Western allies was the Japanese attack on the U.S. fleet at Pearl Harbor in 1941.

TURKS MASSACRE ARMENIANS

> *A Turkish assault on Armenians within the Ottoman Empire killed many and drove survivors to new homes in the United States, the Soviet Union, and other parts of the world.*

Armenian-Turkish Conflict

The Armenian people, who had been converted to Christianity in the fourth century A.D., had once enjoyed political independence. By the beginning of the twentieth century, however, the lands they inhabited were divided among three states: Persia, the Ottoman Empire, and the Empire of the Russian Czars. In each of these states, the Armenians were an ethnic minority.

The Ottoman Armenians lived throughout the eastern half of what is now Turkey in Asia Minor. There were also large Armenian populations in Smyrna (an Aegean seaport), the Syrian cities of Damascus and Aleppo, and the capital city of Constantinople (modern Istanbul). The Armenians looked much like their Turkish neighbors, but there were important cultural differences. The Armenians were Christian, while the Turks were Muslim. The Turks were composed of an illiterate peasant majority ruled by a small elite, while the Armenians had a healthy middle class.

In the second half of the nineteenth century, the Ottoman Armenians became increasingly nationalistic, and many of them came to believe that they should have a state of their own. The Treaty of Berlin, which ended the Russo-Turkish War of 1877-1878, forced the Turks to promise fair treatment of the Armenian Christians within their borders, but set up no practical way of enforcing the promise. The treaty encouraged the Armenians to become bolder and bolder in demanding their rights, while making the Ottoman authorities more and more anxious and resentful.

In 1894-1896, Sultan Abdul-Hamid II, obsessed with the threat of revolution among the

What: Civil strife
When: 1915-1916
Where: The Ottoman Empire (modern Turkey and Syria)
Who:
MEHMET TALAAT PASHA (1872-1921), ENVER PASHA (1881?-1922), and AHMED DJEMAL PASHA (1872-1922), members of the Young Turk triumvirate that ruled the Ottoman Empire from 1913 to 1918
DJEVDET BEY (dates unknown), Turkish Governor of Van in 1915
MUSTAFA KEMAL, later KEMAL ATATÜRK (1881-1938), a Turkish nationalist who founded the Turkish Republic in 1923

Armenians, had 300,000 of them massacred. Although the killings aroused a cry of indignation throughout the United States and Western Europe, disagreements among the Great Powers prevented anything from being done to help the Armenians.

In July, 1908, a military uprising by officers loyal to the underground Committee of Union and Progress (the so-called Young Turks) forced Abdul-Hamid II to give the empire a liberal constitution, with a representative parliament. Yet the Balkan Wars of 1912-1913 put an end to the Young Turks' dream of reviving the Ottoman Empire through liberal, constitutional government. Under the treaty that ended the war, the Ottoman Empire lost Albania, Macedonia, and

Western Thrace. By the thousands, Turkish Muslim refugees from these lost territories poured into Constantinople.

The shock of defeat enraged many Young Turks and destroyed their liberal idealism. There was another coup in January, 1913, and the Turkish cabinet gradually came to be dominated by three Young Turks: War Minister Enver Pasha, Navy Minister Ahmed Djemal Pasha, and Interior Minister Mehmet Talaat Pasha. In the fall of 1914, this group committed the Ottoman Empire to war against Russia, Great Britain, and France on the side of Germany.

The war did not go well for the Turks. They suffered some early defeats, and though they managed to turn back the Allied invasion of Gallipoli, their losses in that campaign were heavy.

Attack on Armenians

Fearing military defeat, the Young Turk triumvirate decided to strike out against the group they saw as the enemy within the gates: the Armenian minority. The Armenians were seen as allied with Russia. An Armenian revolt in the town of Van was seen as proof: Enraged by the brutality of Governor Djevdet Bey, the Armenians in Van rose up against the Turkish authorities on April 20, 1915. On May 16, after much hard fighting, the Armenians were rescued when the Russian Army captured the town from the Turks.

The Ottoman rulers' response was swift. Under the direction of Talaat Pasha, Armenians began to be forced to leave the Ottoman lands. Throughout eastern Anatolia, Armenian men of military age were rounded up, marched off for several miles, and shot. Armenian women, children, and old

men were ordered, at bayonet point, to leave their home villages and move to relocation centers in the Syrian desert.

No effort was made to provide these forced emigrants with food, water, or shelter, and thousands of them dropped dead of hunger, thirst, exhaustion, or disease during the long march to Syria. Many of them were murdered. Survivors were sometimes raped or forced to convert to Islam.

The deportations began in April, 1915, in Cilicia, a Mediterranean coastal province, and spread into other provinces through October. On August 4, Van was recaptured from the Russians. Only in Smyrna and in Constantinople were most of the Armenians spared. On a few occasions groups of Armenians were able to mount an armed resistance, but generally the Turkish Army and police had superior power.

By the beginning of 1916, the deportations had been mostly completed, but occasional outbreaks of violence against Armenians continued until the Turks signed an armistice with the Allies on October 30, 1918. The exact number of Armenians killed through deportations and massacres will never be known; it seems likely that about one million perished.

Consequences

Embroiled in its great war against the Allies, Germany had been unwilling to risk losing Turkish support by pressuring for an end to the persecution of Armenians. Within the United States, however, reports from American diplomats and Protestant missionaries in the Ottoman Empire led to an outpouring of support for the Armenian cause. Money was raised to aid the survivors, and in 1918 former missionary James Barton helped organize the American Committee for the Independence of Armenia, a lobbying group. Its goal was that a state of Greater Armenia be created out of the ruins of the Ottoman Empire.

The Young Turk triumvirate was forced to flee to exile in Germany, and Russian Armenians had organized a small but independent republic of their own. Yet the Soviet Republic of Armenia's hopes for annexing additional territory eventually came to nothing. Military hero Mustafa Kemal came to power over the Turks, and he refused to give up eastern Anatolian territory to the Armenians. Now that World War I was over, the Allied powers were reluctant to become involved in further fighting. In 1919, Kemal's forces entered Smyrna — which had been occupied by the Greek Army — and slaughtered many Armenians in that city.

After 1921, many Armenian survivors of the 1915-1916 massacre migrated to Syria and Lebanon, which had become protectorates of France. Others moved to Soviet Armenia and to the United States.

An Armenian child lies dead in a field near Aleppo, Syria. (*Near East Relief, courtesy Library of Congress*)

The Allies Fight Turkey at Gallipoli

> *The long Allied effort to gain control of the Gallipoli peninsula—and use of the important Dardanelles Straits—ended in a costly defeat.*

What: Military conflict
When: February, 1915-January, 1916
Where: The Gallipoli peninsula of Turkey and surrounding waters
Who:
SIR WINSTON CHURCHILL (1874-1965), British First Lord of the Admiralty from 1911 to 1915
SIR JOHN ARBUTHNOT FISHER (1841-1920), British First Sea Lord
VICE ADMIRAL SIR SACKVILLE HAMILTON CARDEN (1857-1930), commander of the British expeditionary fleet
VICE ADMIRAL JOHN MICHAEL DE ROBECK (1862-1928), Carden's replacement
GENERAL SIR IAN STANDISH HAMILTON (1853-1947), commander of the Allied expeditionary army
GENERAL SIR CHARLES CARMICHAEL MONRO (1860-1929), Hamilton's replacement
HORATIO HERBERT KITCHENER, EARL KITCHENER OF KHARTOUM AND OF BROOME (1850-1916), British Secretary of State for War in 1914
ENVER PASHA (1881?-1922), the head of the ruling junta in Turkey
MUSTAFA KEMAL (1881-1938), a Turkish commander
GENERAL OTTO LIMAN VON SANDERS (1855-1929), German adviser to the Turkish Army and commander of Turkish forces in the Dardanelles

The Offensive Begins

The Gallipoli peninsula is a finger of land about sixty miles long and fifteen miles wide, jutting southwestward from European Turkey into the Aegean Sea. The Dardanelles Straits separates this rocky, scrubby peninsula from Asiatic Turkey and connects the Mediterranean to the entrances to the Black Sea.

When Turkey entered World War I on the side of the Central Powers in late 1914, one of its first moves was to close the Dardanelles to Allied traffic. This was done to keep Russia from receiving arms from its Western allies, Great Britain and France, and to prevent Russia from exporting wheat to the West.

Soon military leaders in Great Britain were debating whether to send in battleships to reopen the Dardanelles. Sir John Fisher warned that the Dardanelles would be strongly defended and that a large number of ships would probably be lost in the effort to force a passage. Sir Winston Churchill and others, however, overcame his arguments. Forcing the Dardanelles would secure the supply line to Russia; an Allied front in the Balkans could be established; Bulgaria would be won to the Allied side; Serbia would be saved; and Constantinople could be attacked, which might knock Turkey out of the war.

Vice Admiral Sir Sackville Hamilton Carden would command the proposed attack. He drew up a plan for destroying the Turkish defenses at the Dardanelles' western entrance, then moving up the forty-mile channel. A major challenge would be to break through the Narrows, a tight neck of the channel that was heavily protected by land

Australian troops charging near a Turkish trench. (*National Archives*)

artillery. If the Allied ships were successful, they could move on to bomb Constantinople.

The French government agreed to send a squadron of ships to join the British fleet. Vice Admiral Carden would command fifteen British battleships, five French battleships, seven Allied cruisers, and various smaller vessels. It would be one of the greatest Allied naval efforts of World War I.

The Turks and their German advisers, meanwhile, had been busily improving the land defenses on both sides of the straits. Mines were placed along the straits, along with antisubmarine nets, searchlights, and torpedoes.

Allied ships began bombarding Turkish forts on the western approach in the early morning of February 19, 1915. After several hours, the Turk-ish defenders withdrew from the outer forts, and marines were sent in to destroy the abandoned guns.

About a week later, the Allied fleet moved forward again. Mine-sweeping trawlers were sent ahead to clear a channel through the mine fields. Meanwhile, the Turks strengthened the forts at the Narrows. Ill and exhausted, Vice Admiral Carden returned home; he was replaced by Vice Admiral John Michael de Robeck.

On March 5, the Allies attacked the Narrows' forts and succeeded in smashing Fort Chanak on the Asiatic side. Yet the Allies did suffer serious losses. Of the fifty-eight Allied ships in the Narrows engagement, about a dozen were lost on the afternoon of March 5, and some two thousand men died.

Still, Lord Herbert Kitchener, British Secretary of State for War, joined Churchill in urging Robeck to push forward through the Narrows. The Turks and Germans expected the British to continue trying, but Robeck decided that naval action would not be enough to gain control of the Dardanelles; the forts would have to be defeated by the Allied army. He withdrew the Allied fleet from the Narrows.

The Land Battles

General Ian Hamilton had been appointed commander of an Allied expeditionary force consisting of British and French soldiers. It took some time for all the forces to arrive and for landing craft to be assembled and transports to be repacked. The Turks used the delay to improve the Gallipoli defenses. Turkish leader Enver Pasha and Otto Liman von Sanders, German commander of the Turkish forces in the Dardanelles, raised six divisions of soldiers and put them at strategic points on the peninsula.

The first British landings on Gallipoli were made from Lemnos on April 25, at Cape Helles and Ari Burnu. The French landed at Kum-Kale, on the Asiatic side of the entrance to the Dardanelles. They soon joined the British forces on the peninsula. Turkish artillery on the Gallipoli heights kept up a heavy fire against the invaders. Several of the landing parties were driven back off the beaches, but other groups were able to establish their position on beachheads along Gallipoli's southwestern edge.

By early May, 1915, the Allies had about seventy thousand troops on the western end of Gallipoli. They moved eastward toward the village of Krithia, which controlled the only road through the peninsula. The fight for Krithia was very intense, and the Allies finally had to pull back when their ammunition ran out. A week later, they tried again. The British took about half of the village, but then a little-known commander of a Turkish reserve brigade, Mustafa Kemal, led his men to drive the British back again.

Both sides then settled into trench warfare, bombarding each other across the width of the peninsula. The slaughter and the suffering were terrible. The British suffered from a scarcity of fresh water, which had to be brought ashore by ships. Malaria and dysentery struck down hundreds of soldiers, and the battle was in a stalemate.

Hamilton decided to break the deadlock by attempting a landing at Suvla Bay, on the peninsula's north shore. More Allied troops were brought in, along with stocks of ammunition.

At Suvla Bay, Australian and New Zealand troops and Indian Ghurkas went in first. They got ashore on August 6 and headed for the twelve-hundred-foot ridges called Sari Bair. On the way, they had to cross a wide, flat beach protected by Turkish guns on the cliffs above. The Allied troops were hit hard as they advanced, but some of them reached the Sari Bair crests.

Then the Turks, led by Kemal, counterattacked to drive the Allied forces off the crests. Again, the losses on both sides were heavy. Finally, the Allied attackers were forced to withdraw to the beaches. The Allied offensive had failed.

General Hamilton was relieved of his command. Allied armies still held points around Gallipoli's perimeter, but they were not strong enough to return to the offensive. In November, 1915, the new commander, General Charles Monro, recommended that the troops be withdrawn. The withdrawal began the following month and finished in January, 1916.

Consequences

Gallipoli was a serious defeat for the British. The human costs were enormous: Each side lost more than 250,000 men. There were consequences, too, for various British leaders. Churchill was forced out of office, Fisher resigned, and Hamilton left the army.

On the Turkish side, Mustafa Kemal was hailed as the "Savior of Gallipoli." He went on to become the first president of the Turkish Republic.

> *Though Italy had at first declared neutrality in World War I, British and French promises of new territories helped to propel it into the conflict on the Allied side.*

Objections to Neutrality

When World War I broke out in the Balkans, Italy announced its decision to remain neutral. At this time, it was a member of the Central Powers (which had also been known as the Triple Alliance) and might have been expected to join forces with Germany and Austria-Hungary. Yet Italian leaders argued that when Austria declared war on Serbia, it was not acting defensively. Therefore Italy was not under obligation to support Austria in the conflict.

Italy's position, announced by the conservative government of Antonio Salandra in Rome, was at first favored by many Italians. Those who supported neutrality included most of the Socialist Party, the liberal-democrat Giovanni Giolitti and a number of other parliamentarians, and the Roman Catholic clergy.

Yet voices favoring involvement on the side of the Allies (the Triple Entente) began to be heard more and more. Older liberals in Italy tended to see France and Great Britain as leaders of civilized world development, and they believed that Italy would be wise to ally itself with them. The Italian army and the press favored intervention; their spokespersons included a Socialist editor named Benito Mussolini and a well-known nationalist poet named Gabriele D'Annunzio.

D'Annunzio and other Italian nationalists wanted to see their nation restored to unity and to a position of international strength and respect. D'Annunzio's efforts to get Italy involved in the war were especially effective. His arguments persuaded many Italians who had originally been undecided, and the result was mass demonstra-

What: Military conflict
When: May, 1915
Where: Rome
Who:
ANTONIO SALANDRA (1853-1931), Premier of Italy from 1914 to 1916
GIOVANNI GIOLITTI (1842-1928), a leading liberal-democrat in Italy's Chamber of Deputies
GABRIELE D'ANNUNZIO (1863-1938), a poet and Italian nationalist
BENITO MUSSOLINI (1883-1945), a Socialist editor

tions in the streets of Rome, calling for an Italian war commitment.

Negotiations with the Allies

Diplomats representing both sides of the war had been busy in Rome, each group trying to win the Italian government to its side. The Allies were pleased at first with Italy's neutrality—and became even more pleased when the Italian people began calling openly for involvement on the Allied side.

Salandra's government, however, insisted that if Italy were to join the war effort, it should be promised generous rewards. Talks between the Italian and the Allied governments focused on this issue. The British and the French were willing to guarantee an array of new territories for Italy.

The British and French offers included many areas in southeastern Europe and the eastern Mediterranean. The Allies promised that Italy

133

would receive the Austrian Tyrol as far north as the Brenner Pass; Trieste; a number of Adriatic regions, including northern Albania; and, if Turkey were to be divided up, a piece of Asia Minor. In addition, a share of the war-reparations funds from the defeated Central Powers would come to Italy.

With such lavish promises, Italy's commitment to neutrality began to weaken, and the government became more open to intervening in the war. Italian leaders were especially interested in acquiring territories inhabited by people of Italian origin. Control over wider regions to its north and the Adriatic Sea communities to the east would put Italy in the position of influencing Mediterranean affairs.

By the spring of 1915, the only remaining obstacles were the Church, the Socialist Party, and the supporters of Giolitti in the Chamber of Deputies. Giolitti, the leading Italian liberal-democrat since the turn of the century, remained determined to oppose Italian involvement in the war, but most of his allies were not as determined. Street mobs in Rome were already shouting their objections to Giolitti's position, and both the Church and the Socialists were intimidated by public opinion. Without strong backing for his position, Giolitti's efforts to preserve neutrality were doomed.

On May 18, 1915, Salandra's government offered the Chamber of Deputies a war resolution. On April 26, 1915, a secret treaty had already been signed in London with Great Britain and France. This treaty promised Italy many territorial rewards and part of the war-reparations money. With these guarantees, the war resolution passed easily; only a few Giolitti loyalists voted against it. In May, Italy formally entered the war by declaring war on Austria-Hungary.

Consequences

Italy's military contribution to the Allied war effort proved to be fairly small. The country's armed forces were not prepared to create any major threat to Germany and Austria-Hungary, and the Italians were unable to keep the Central Powers from overrunning Romania.

At the end of World War I, United States President Woodrow Wilson's Fourteen Points were influential in the drafting of the Treaty of Versailles. Wilson stressed that the war should be ended in a spirit of restoration, not punishment.

As a result, Italy failed to receive all the territories that had been promised in the Treaty of London. The Italian people's resentment over the conclusion of the war combined with turmoil inside the country to encourage the rise of Fascism under Benito Mussolini.

In the trenches near San Marco during action of May 12, 1917. (*Library of Congress*)

THE UNIVERSAL NEGRO IMPROVEMENT ASSOCIATION IS FOUNDED

Marcus Garvey's emphasis on black pride and self-help was a major contribution to race consciousness in the United States.

What: Civil rights and social reform
When: 1916
Where: Harlem, New York
Who:
MARCUS MOZIAH GARVEY (1887-1940), the founder of the Universal Negro Improvement Association
BOOKER TALIAFERRO WASHINGTON (1856-1915), an African-American educator
DUSE MOHAMMED (dates unknown), an African scholar in London

Garvey's Work Begins

Marcus Garvey was born in St. Ann's Bay, Jamaica, in 1887. He later claimed to be of pure African descent. His father was a descendant of the Maroons, or Jamaican slaves, who successfully revolted against their British masters in 1739.

During his early years, Garvey gradually realized that his color was a badge of inferiority. In Jamaica, the mulattoes (mixed-race blacks with light skin) had higher status than dark-skinned blacks. Though Garvey grew up with a sense of isolation, he also came to take pride in his color.

By his twentieth birthday, Garvey had started a program to change the lives of blacks in Jamaica. While working as a foreman in a printing shop in 1907, he became a leader in a labor strike. The strike was quickly broken by the shop owners, however, and as a result Garvey lost faith in labor unions as a way to bring about social reform.

In 1910, he began publishing a newspaper, the *Watchman*, and helped form a political organization called the National Club. These efforts were not especially successful either, but they did inspire Garvey to visit Central America, where he was able to observe the miserable conditions of blacks in Costa Rica and Panama.

Garvey's travels eventually led him to London, the center of the British Empire. There he met Duse Mohammed, an African scholar who increased the young Jamaican's knowledge and awareness of Africa. During this time, Garvey also read Booker T. Washington's *Up from Slavery* (1901), which acquainted him with the problems of African Americans. Reading Washington's autobiography raised questions in Garvey's mind: "I asked, where is the black man's Government? Where is his President, his country and his ambassador, his army, his navy, his men of big affairs? I could not find them, and then I declared, I will help to make them."

Returning to Jamaica in 1914, Garvey started a self-help organization for black people and called it the Universal Negro Improvement and Conservation Association and African Communities League. This new organization, whose name was soon shortened to the Universal Negro Improvement Association (UNIA), called for the union of "all people of Negro or African parentage." The goals of the UNIA were to increase racial pride, aid black people throughout the world, and "establish a central nation for the race."

Garvey, who was elected the first president of

Marcus Garvey. (*Library of Congress*)

the UNIA, realized that black people would have to achieve these goals without help from white people. This self-help concept, which resembled the ideas of Booker T. Washington, led Garvey to propose a trade school for blacks in Kingston, Jamaica, similar to Washington's Tuskegee Institute. Yet he was not able to gather much support for the plan.

Garvey in America

In 1915, Garvey decided to come to the United States to seek aid for his organization. He exchanged letters with Washington, but Washington died before Garvey arrived in the United States in 1916. Garvey went immediately to Harlem, which in the early twentieth century was gaining a large population of African Americans.

The lives of African Americans were changing rapidly during these years. Cities in the North were receiving mass migrations of blacks from the South. In New York City, for example, the population of African Americans increased from 91,709 in 1910, to 152,467 in 1920. They were attracted by the promise of jobs and by the possibility of escaping the rigid system of segregation in the South.

Yet they found that they could not escape racism simply by moving north. Northern whites believed in the racial inferiority of blacks just as Southern whites did, and they resented having to compete with African Americans for jobs. Like immigrants from abroad, the new African-American residents were crowded in ghettos without proper housing. Racial violence broke out in several Northern cities.

The people of Harlem were not particularly interested in Booker T. Washington's philosophy, which they saw as giving in too much to the white power structure, and the National Association for the Advancement of Colored People seemed too intellectual and middle-class. Yet Garvey was able to attract support from the Jamaican immigrants in Harlem, who felt isolated, and he established a branch of the UNIA there in 1916.

At first, the organization met with serious problems. Local politicians tried to gain control of it, and Garvey had to struggle hard to keep the UNIA's independence. The original branch of the UNIA was dissolved, and a charter was obtained from the State of New York which prevented other groups from using the organization's name.

By 1918, under Garvey's leadership, the New York chapter of the UNIA had 3,500 members. By 1919, Garvey claimed two million members for his organization across the world and 200,000 subscribers for his publication, *Negro World*.

To help blacks economically, in 1916 Garvey set up two joint-stock companies—the Black Star Line, an international commercial shipping company, and the Negro Factories Corporation, which was to build and run factories "to manufacture every marketable commodity." Stock in these companies was sold only to blacks. The Black Star Line was to establish trade with Africa and to transport willing blacks to a new community in Africa. Although both companies failed financially, their existence gave many blacks a feeling of dignity.

Consequences

At the urging of rival African-American leaders, the U.S. government had Garvey indicted for fraudulent use of the mails in 1922. He was tried, found guilty, and sent to prison in 1923. The UNIA began to lose its organizational strength.

In 1927, Garvey was released from prison and deported as an "undesirable alien." He returned to Jamaica and then went to London and Paris, where he tried to resurrect the UNIA, but met with little success. He died in poverty in London in 1940.

Although he failed as a businessman, Garvey was an eloquent spokesman for African Americans and other blacks throughout the world. His speeches and writings contributed to the development of racial awareness and pride among African Americans.

CHRONOLOGICAL LIST OF EVENTS

I

IV

V

GREAT EVENTS

VIII

X

XIV

XVI

XVII

CATEGORY INDEX

XX

MILITARY REFORM. *See* MILITARY CAPABILITY *and* POLITICS
    AND POLITICAL REFORM

NATIONAL POLITICS

POLITICAL AGGRESSION. *See* CIVIL STRIFE *and* MILITARY
    CONFLICT

SOCIAL CHANGE

TECHNOLOGY AND TECHNOLOGICAL ADVANCE. *See also*
    MILITARY CAPABILITY

WAR. *See* CIVIL WAR *and* MILITARY CONFLICT

GEOGRAPHICAL INDEX

XXXIX

XL

I

Discard